D1486364

# The Economy under Mrs Thatcher

UNIVERSITY OF
**WOLVERHAMPTON**
KNOWLEDGE • INNOVATION • ENTERPRISE

First published 1988
Reprinted 1989

Basil Blackwell Ltd
108 Cowley Road, Oxford OX4 1JF, UK

Basil Blackwell Inc.
3 Cambridge Center
Cambridge, Massachusetts 02142, USA

*British Library Cataloguing in Publication Data*

Maynard, Geoffrey
  The economy under Mrs Thatcher.
  1. Great Britain, Economic conditions
  I. Title
  330.941 0858
  ISBN 0−631−15875−8
  ISBN 0−631−15874−X Pbk

*Library of Congress Cataloging in Publication Data*

Maynard, Geoffrey.
  The economy under Mrs Thatcher.
  1. Great Britain—Economic policy—1945−
  2. Great Britain—Economic conditions—1945−
  I. Title.
  HC256.6.M39    1988      338.941    88−4343
  ISBN 0−631−15875−8
  ISBN 0−631−15874−X (pbk.)

Typeset on 10½ on 11½ pt Times
by Colset Private Limited, Singapore
Printed in Great Britain by T.J. Press (Padstow) Ltd, Padstow, Cornwall

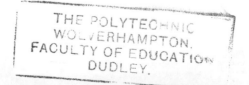

# 1

# Economic Policy and Performance prior to Thatcher

## The Policy Model

Prior to Mrs Thatcher, macroeconomic policy in the UK was rooted in John Maynard Keynes's *General Theory of Employment, Interest and Money*,[1] although, as will be suggested later, interpretation of the message of that great book and translation into specific areas of policy probably did less than justice to it. Implicit in UK policy therefore was the presumption that an unregulated capitalist economy was prone to instability, owing to fluctuations in the prospective return to capital (in Keynesian terms, the marginal efficiency of capital) and also prone to 'involuntary' unemployment owing to lack of equality between *ex ante* private sector investment and saving (a deficiency of demand) at full employment level of income. In other words there could be insufficient demand to absorb all the output that could be produced if the working force was fully employed. Moreover, in line with Keynes's own thinking, policy makers were doubtful that the free working of labour and commodity markets *per se* could be relied upon to restore full employment output, at least in any short period of time, so that macroeconomic policy was necessary to offset such fluctuations and inequalities. Thus implicitly a Keynesian income and expenditure model lay at the centre of policy making.[2]

1 Macmillan, London 1936.
2 In this brief review of the main lines of economic policy prior to Thatcher, no attempt is made to distinguish between the policies of Conservative and Labour governments since a broad acceptance of Keynesian policies

In this model, as relied upon in UK policy making, money played little or no role, at any rate until the 1970s.[3] The demand for money[4] was taken to be rather interest rate elastic (so that manipulation of the quantity of money in so far as this was possible, had relatively small effects on interest rates), whilst the interest rate elasticity of expenditure on goods and services was assumed to be low so that what interest rate changes did take place had small effect on expenditure. Hence monetary policy was viewed as generally impotent for controlling economic activity (although various forms of credit control and credit rationing were employed);[5] and fiscal policy – the manipulation of the level of government expenditure and the balance between expenditure and taxation, i.e. the budget surplus or deficit – was assigned the chief macroeconomic policy role.[6,7]

---

and objectives was common to all. A possible exception is the Conservative government of 1970–4 led by Mr Heath, which initially attempted to introduce many of the radical changes later adopted by Mrs Thatcher; but Mr Heath was soon forced into a U-turn, leaving behind rampant inflation and overweening trade union power. For a comparison of the governments of Mr Heath and Mrs Thatcher, see D. Kavanagh's contribution to *Ruling Performance*, ed. P. Hennessey and A. Seldon (Blackwell, Oxford, 1987).

3 This doesn't mean that monetary policy was not employed: interest rates were often raised sharply and hire purchase controls tightened at times of balance of payments crises. But short term manipulation of money supply was not seen as a means, along with fiscal policy, of fine tuning the economy; and certainly no target for long run monetary growth was envisaged.

4 The demand for money here means the desire of the general public – households and firms – to hold their *financial* wealth in the form of money, rather than in, say, bonds or equities. The problem of defining 'money' is discussed in later chapters.

5 For example, control of hire purchase financing. Emphasis on 'credit' rather than on 'money' has always been a feature of UK monetary policy.

6 In fact, Keynes seems to have put more emphasis on public works as a means of creating employment than on deficit financing *per se*. Moreover, his emphasis on public works as against expansionary monetary policy may have reflected a lack of confidence not in the impact of interest rates on spending but rather in his belief that in the 1930s interest rates were at their 'liquidity preference' minimum. See H. Rose, 'Another look at the inter-war period', *Barclay's Review*, 58/1 (Feb. 1983).

7 It should be noted that in the 1930s the so-called 'Treasury view' was highly sceptical of Keynesian remedies for unemployment, believing that government spending on public works etc. would result in 'crowding out' and/or balance of payments difficulties. See Committee on Finance of

Apart from this income–expenditure core to policy making, UK policy was based on other assumptions thought to be of a Keynesian nature or apparently supported by empirical evidence. It was taken for granted that, at the aggregate level at any rate, an excess supply of goods and an excess supply of labour were largely synonymous, i.e. unemployment of labour was due to deficiency of aggregate demand for goods – hence if significant unemployment appeared, an expansion of aggregate demand for goods was an appropriate policy response, subject to the constraint of inflation. But prices and money wages were seen to be determined largely but not wholly independently of the demand for goods and labour, so that inflation bore more the characteristics of cost push than excess demand. This view was modified by discovery of an apparent empirical relationship between inflation and unemployment (the Phillips curve)[8] which suggested a trade-off between the two (i.e. less unemployment could be obtained at the expense of more inflation); but while this relationship was taken some account of when determining appropriate levels of aggregate demand, policy makers were more inclined to resort to incomes policies for reconciling high employment and reasonable price stability.

Incomes policies constitute an attempt to replace market determination of wage behaviour with administrative targets or controls, and they operated extensively throughout the 1960s and 1970s, in a variety of forms (see table 1.1). In some periods they were voluntary; at other times compulsory. Exceptional pay awards were sometimes allowed outside a pay increase norm or freeze; at other times, not. Usually the policy-on period was of short duration, often lasting little more than a year; but the policy-off periods were equally short. The longest period of non-market restraint, 1974–8, was associated with a so-called 'Social Contract' between government and trade unions but this ended in bitter industrial conflict (the winter of discontent) which helped to bring down the (Labour) government. The evidence suggests that while incomes

Industry (the Macmillan) Report, 1930. See also chapter 2 of this book for a discussion of 'crowding out'.

8 A.W. Phillips, 'The relation between unemployment and the rate of change of money wages in the UK, 1861–1957', *Economica*, 25 (1958). The so-called Phillips curve has been the subject of intense debate and research and detailed references cannot be provided here. A useful early exposition can be found in R.G. Lipsey, *Economica* (n.s.), 27 (Feb. 1960). See also G. Maynard and W. van Ryckeghem, *A World of Inflation* (Batsford, London, 1976), ch. 7, for an empirical testing of the relationship in the OECD countries.

**Table 1.1**    Incomes policies, 1961–77

| Policy period | Pay restrictions | Implementation | Conditions |
|---|---|---|---|
| 1961–2 | Zero norm | Voluntary | Existing commitments honoured |
| 1962–3 | 2–2.5 % then 3–3 % | Voluntary | (i) Exceptional productivity (ii) Labour mobility (iii) Certain differential adjustment in the national interest |
| 1965–6 | 3–3.5 % | Voluntary | As above plus provisions for low pay |
| 1966–7 | Freeze for 6 months Zero norm | Compulsory for freeze | |
| 1967–8 | Zero norm | Voluntary but with powers of delay | (i) to (iv) of stage 1 above |
| 1968–9 | Zero norm | Voluntary but with powers of delay | 3.5 % average increase as a ceiling for exceptional cases. No ceiling on productivity bargaining, wage differentials and low paid workers |
| 1969–70 | 2.5–4.5 % | Voluntary but with powers of delay | As above but no 3.5 % ceiling |
| 1971–2 | $(n-1)$ policy | Voluntary (government example: public sector) | None |
| 1972–3 | Freeze | Compulsory | None |

Nor was the supply side of the economy explicitly modelled: that is to say, no explicit regard was paid to the relationship between such factors as technology, or to relative amounts of capital, labour and other inputs employed (a function of their relative prices) on the one hand, and output on the other – the so-called production function.[13] Neither the demand for labour nor the supply of it was expressed as a function of the price of labour, so that employment was seen to be determined by output which was solely determined by real expenditure. If real wages entered the model, they did so via their influence on aggregate demand for goods, rather than as a variable entering directly into labour demand and supply functions.

It can of course be contended that the proof of the pudding is in the eating. On the face of it, if unemployment and the rate of inflation are to be the judge, policy was rather successful in the 1950s and 1960s. Unemployment averaged less than 2 per cent and inflation barely 3 per cent per annum while the balance of payments was troublesome rather than serious. Overall performance was marred by a rather low real growth rate as compared with other major industrial countries[14] but this was seen to reflect underlying sociological characteristics of the UK economy rather than the outcome of macroeconomic policy *per se*.

## 1950s and 1960s: a Favourable Environment

However, it has been argued that the high level of activity and employment enjoyed by European economies, including the UK, in the post Second World War period had nothing, or at any rate little, to do with

---

attempted to reconcile the classical economists' emphasis on saving and investment as the determinants of the rate of interest with Keynes's emphasis on the demand and supply of money. For an excellent exposition of the analysis which emerged from this article and which formed the basis of much of post-Keynesian macroeconomic analysis, see D. Laidler, 'The influence of money on economic activity: a survey of some current problems', in G. Clayton, J. C. Gilbert, and R. Sedgwick (eds), *Monetary Theory and Policy in the 1970s* (Oxford University Press, 1986).

13 The fact that in the *General Theory* Keynes assumed a fixed capital stock and a fixed stock of labour, was no excuse for policy makers to make similar assumptions.

14 A. Maddison, *Phases of Capitalist Development* (Oxford University Press 1982).

the Keynesian macroeconomic policies that were pursued[15]. It would certainly seem that, from our present viewpoint, the 1950s and 1960s presented a rather special environment conducive to relative macro-economic stability in the industrial countries. Unlike the 1930s, the need to rebuild all war-torn economies of Europe and elsewhere precluded the possibility of a deficiency of investment (capital formation) in relation to saving, which in any case was held down by the desire of households to return to pre-war standards of living. A sustained deficiency of demand seemed unlikely. Moreover, in other respects it was an environment in which the Treasury macro-model referred to earlier provided a reasonable guide to short term UK policy and its outcome.[16] For example, it was a period of *fixed* (but adjustable) exchange rates: thus the Bank of England had little or no control over money supply so that of necessity fiscal policy had to be the main instrument for controlling domestic economic activity.[17] Moreover, the UK inflation rate was closely tied to the world inflation rate, which was determined by US monetary policy, and this remained generally conservative and responsible at least until the second half of the 1960s.[18] Also, following

15 R.C.O. Mathews, 'Why has Britain had full employment since the War', *Economic Journal* (Sept. 1968).

16 The 'thought model' is referred to here rather than the formal econometric model, since the latter was not developed until the late 1960s or early 1970s.

17 An attempt by the Bank of England to restrict domestic money supply would tend to raise UK interest rates relative to interest rates overseas. Foreign capital would tend to be attracted into the UK, so keeping up money supply. The attempt to increase money supply would have opposite effects. However, prior to 1979, the UK employed foreign exchange controls over movements of capital so that the Bank of England had some control.

18 In the so-called Bretton Woods international monetary system which provided the regime for exchange rate management from 1945 to 1971, central banks intervened in foreign exchange markets by buying and selling their national currencies in exchange for the US dollar at a rate that was allowed to fluctuate within only very narrow margins around an agreed or pegged level. This pegged level or rate could be changed by agreement if a country found it difficult to maintain balance of payments equilibrium consistent with domestic full employment and price stability; but in between such adjustments, which were rare, central banks other than the Federal Reserve in the US had effectively abandoned control over their domestic money supplies: they had to create or extinguish domestic money to keep the exchange rate against the dollar at or close to the agreed rate. Although there was a constraint on the Federal Reserve in the US, exerted by the United States commitment to convert dollars into gold at a fixed price ($35 per fine ounce),

the conclusion of the Korean War in the early 1950s, world commodity prices exhibited a declining trend through most of the next two decades, and the terms of trade of industrial countries generally improved (see figure 1.1). Not only was this conducive to overall price stability, it provided the basis for a rise in real wages in excess of productivity growth, without the compression of profits that would otherwise have occurred.

This favourable environment disappeared at the end of the 1960s with the collapse of the Bretton Woods international monetary system.[19] The circumstances of that collapse produced a worldwide burst of inflation in which the terms of trade of industrial countries massively worsened. Although the rise in non-oil commodity prices was quickly reversed, a quadrupling of oil prices in 1973–4 prevented any comparable decline in raw material input price to manufacturing industry; moreover, a wage–price spiral had been set in motion which could not be easily contained. The impact of these factors affected prices and balances of payments differently for different countries, and stability of exchange rates proved impossible. By 1973 the world had moved to a floating exchange rate system, and an era of high inflation had been ushered in.[20]

Floating exchange rates and relative high inflation rates (as compared with the 1950s and 1960s) had considerable implications for macroeconomic policy, both in theory and in practice. In the first place floating exchange rates meant the reversal of roles for monetary and fiscal policy. If central banks refrained from intervening in exchange markets, then they could in principle control domestic money supply and therefore hope to influence domestic economic activity and the price level. On the other hand, fiscal policy without accommodating monetary policy would now be impotent for influencing domestic economic activity, since changes in the stance of fiscal policy unaccompanied by monetary change in the same direction would simply bring about changes in the interest rate and the exchange rate, offsetting the

---

Federal Reserve policy effectively determined world money supply and therefore the world inflation rate. See B. Tew, *The Evolution of the International Monetary System 1945–77* (Hutchinson, 1977) or any other textbook on international monetary economics for an account of the origin of the system and a description of its operation.

19  The US brought about the collapse in 1971 by withdrawing its commitment to convert dollars into gold.

20  See G. Maynard and W. van Ryckeghem, *A World of Inflation*, ch. 10 for a short discussion of the events and consequences of this period.

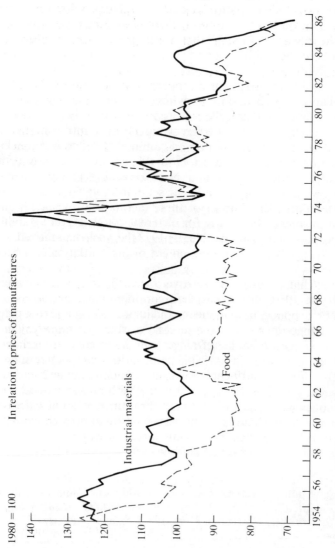

**Figure 1.1** Real commodity prices

*Source:* Financial Statement and Budget Report, 1987–8, (HM Treasury, March 1987)

primary influence of the fiscal change. Fiscal expansion, for example, would tend to force up interest rates and therefore the exchange rate, so curtailing private sector demand as public sector expenditure rose. It was perhaps as much the transition to floating exchange rates as the blandishments of Milton Friedman that caused governments to become monetarist.

High inflation also appeared to affect some basic macroeconomic relationships. It led to the decline of 'money illusion', a condition in which transactors do not distinguish between changes in money values and changes in real values when making spending or other decisions. Given low inflation, the cost of money illusion is probably negligible, but with high inflation the cost becomes serious. Decline of money illusion is particularly serious in wage bargaining and price fixing – since expectations of future price and wage behaviour can now enter, so that inflation can become self-generating.

Moreover, inflation seems to have changed some real relationships (i.e., relationships between real variables), or at any rate revealed that earlier equations linking some real relationships had been misspecified or misunderstood. For example, in the 1970s a considerable shift in the consumption function, i.e. a relationship between real income and real consumption, seems to have occurred in most European countries. Real consumption as a proportion of real disposable income, both on average and at the margin, seems to have fallen. It is not absolutely certain that inflation alone was the cause of this shift – unemployment may have been a separate factor underlying an increase in precautionary saving – but it is clear that the impact of unexpected inflation on the real value of liquid assets held by persons or firms could be a factor inducing them to save a larger proportion of their incomes in order to restore the real value of those assets. Thus the construction of macroeconomic policy models became difficult and their use for economic policy making more hazardous.

## Resort to Floating Exchange Rates

Although the UK policy makers had been convinced of the virtues of fixed exchange rates in the 1950s and 1960s, and although they were forced into floating sterling in June 1972 as a result of a serious currency crisis (rather than doing so as a deliberate choice), they soon accepted the new regime with enthusiasm although, it might be thought, with less than full appreciation of the implications – and with unfortunate results. The Conservative administration under Mr Heath had come to power in June 1970 full of determination to raise the UK's real growth rate and to escape from the 'stop–go' policies of the previous two decades. Floating the exchange rate (which some academics and financial journalists had long been urging the government to do) seemed to provide escape from balance of payments constraints which, so it had been argued, were the principal cause of the UK's poor real economic performance.

But UK policy makers seemed slow to appreciate the implications of a floating exchange rate for domestic monetary policy. As indicated earlier, a move to a floating exchange rate system tends to increase the relative importance of monetary policy as against fiscal policy as a means of influencing domestic economic activity and prices. In contrast with a fixed exchange rate system, excess domestic credit creation cannot leak abroad since the excess demand for foreign exchange which would be created by it causes the exchange rate to depreciate, thereby choking off the outflow. As a result, domestic economic activity and income are affected rather than the balance of payments. On the other hand, because of the impact of exchange rate depreciation on foreign trade sector prices (both import and export) in domestic currency, excess credit creation tends to have a larger and more immediate impact on the domestic price level than on real economic activity.[21]

In the twelve months following the floating of sterling in June 1972, money supply in the UK, as measured by Sterling M3,[22] increased by 30 per cent, and by another 20 per cent in the next twelve months. Although clearly the introduction of 'Competition and Credit Control' at the end of 1971[23] could have been expected to lead to some reintermediation of the banking system and therefore to a temporary faster growth of commercial bank liabilities, these increases were

21   See G. Maynard, 'Monetary independence and floating exchange rates', in *Monetary Policies in Open Economies* (Société Universitaire Européenne de Récherches Financières, Series 19A, 1978).

22   Sterling M3 is a wide concept of the money supply including Bank of England notes plus coin plus non-interest and interest-bearing sight deposits with commercial banks, plus UK private sector sterling time deposits with banks. Narrower concepts of money are referred to in later chapters.

23   This measure was introduced in 1971 by the then Conservative government led by Mr Heath with the aim of sweeping away existing quantitative and qualitative controls on credit markets. The regime lasted only two years. As a result of the tremendous expansion of money and credit in those years, a new control in the form of a restriction on the expansion of the banking system's 'interest-bearing eligible liabilities' (IBELS) was introduced. This was soon nicknamed 'the corset'.

excessive; and indeed they were the result of the government's reluctance to use interest rates as a means of control, despite the abolition of controls over lending. It is not surprising that the pound's dollar exchange rate fell from $2.60 in June 1972 to around $2.38 in mid 1974, a fall which continued through 1975 (reaching about $2.00 at the end of the year) during which period money supply continued to rise at a fast rate. Nor is it surprising that UK retail prices rose by about 70 per cent during the three years following floating, although of course part of this was due to the worldwide rise in oil and other commodity prices during these years (see below) and part was due to the partial indexing of money wages in the form of 'threshold' payments introduced at the end of 1973 by the then government, in an attempt to get union agreement to wage restraint (see table 1.1). All other countries experienced an acceleration of inflation during these years but few of them suffered as badly as the UK.

Of more significance was the fact that the policy of allowing the exchange rate to float did not unleash real growth potential in the UK: the notion that UK real growth in the 1960s had been held back by a balance of payments constraint was shown to be the illusion one should have expected. Certainly constraints on economic growth existed, but these lay much more in factors governing the supply side performance of the economy. The nature of these constraints became increasingly evident in the 1970s and increasingly influenced the nature and direction of economic policy; but the antecedents were clearly visible in the second half of the 1960s, at least for those who managed to shift their attention from macroeconomic variables and determinants of aggregate demand.

One indication was the growing difficulty experienced by the UK after the mid 1960s in combining balance of payments equilibrium with full employment: each successive cycle in economic activity saw the trade-off between them getting worse – i.e., in booms, balance of payments deficits increasingly got bigger for any given fall in unemployment, whilst in recessions, unemployment got worse for any given improvement in the balance of payments. Another indication was the downward trend in the rate of return on capital employed in British industry, including manufacturing, which fell by more than three quarters from the early 1960s to the end of the 1970s (see figure 1.2 and table 1.2). In part, this was due to the massive rise in the price of oil which deflated the UK economy and the world economy generally.[24]

---

[24] It raised the price level relatively to money incomes in the oil-consuming countries, leading to a deflation of real demand. Thus the rise in the oil price was price inflationary and output deflationary.

The rate of return, having fallen from around 15 per cent since the early 1960s, fell further from 9 per cent in 1973 to barely 4 per cent in 1975. Some recovery in profits then took place as manufacturing prices responded with time-lag to the rise in manufacturing costs, and the profit rate recovered to 7 per cent in 1977. The downward trend was then resumed, so that by 1978 the real return on capital had fallen to barely 3 per cent as against 12 per cent in the mid 1960s.

Falling profit rate, increasing balance of payments difficulties and growing unemployment were not unconnected. There is a temptation to see the connection in an overvalued exchange rate which would have depressed profits and made difficulties for the balance of payments. An overvalued exchange rate may have been a problem in the first half of the 1960s when, against a background of a fixed *nominal* exchange rate, relatively rising labour costs in the UK put upward pressure on the UK's real exchange rate. This would certainly have tended to squeeze profits. But this line of explanation will not do for the faster fall in profits and capital productivity in the late 1960s and early 1970s during which time the depreciation of sterling more than offset the UK's faster rising labour costs. Between the mid 1960s and the mid 1970s UK trade competitiveness, as measured by an index of normalized unit labour costs, improved by about 15 per cent.

### Relative Factor Prices

A clue may be found by decomposing the factors underlying the behaviour of the rate of profit on capital. Algebraically, the rate of profit on capital is the product of the share of profits in income, or value added, and the ratio of output to capital employed (i.e. the productivity of capital or the inverse of the capital–output ratio). The latter ratio can be further decomposed into the ratio of capital to labour and the ratio of output to labour (i.e. the productivity of labour). Putting these ratios together, we see that the rate of profit on capital is positively related to the share of profits in income and to the productivity of labour, but negatively related to the ratio of capital to labour.[25] Table 1.2 indicates that a major factor underlying the fall in the net rate of

25 Let P = profit, K = stock of capital, Y = output (value added), L = labour employed. Then $\frac{P}{K} = \frac{P}{Y} \cdot \frac{Y}{K} = \frac{P}{Y} \cdot \frac{Y}{L} \cdot \frac{L}{K}$

**Table 1.2**   UK pre-tax profitability, 1955–84

|  | Non-financial corporations | Industry plus transport | Manufacturing industry |
|---|---|---|---|
| (a) *Net real rate of return on fixed capital* | | | |
| 1955–8 | 13 | 10 | 16 |
| 1959–62 | 12 | 10 | 14 |
| 1963–7 | 11 | 10 | 12 |
| 1968–71 | 8 | 9 | 10 |
| 1972–5 | 6 | 7 | 8 |
| 1976–80 | 6 | 7 | 6 |
| (b) *Net profit share in value added* | | | |
| 1955–8 | 23 | 22 | 24 |
| 1959–62 | 22 | 22 | 22 |
| 1963–7 | 22 | 22 | 20 |
| 1968–71 | 19 | 21 | 18 |
| 1972–5 | 15 | 18 | 15 |
| 1976 | 16 | 20 | 13 |
| (c) *Implied ratio of capital to output* | | | |
| 1955–8 | 1.76 | 2.2 | 1.50 |
| 1959–62 | 1.83 | 2.2 | 1.57 |
| 1963–7 | 2.00 | 2.2 | 1.66 |
| 1968–71 | 2.37 | 2.33 | 1.80 |
| 1972–5 | 2.50 | 2.57 | 1.75 |
| 1976–80 | 2.66 | 2.85 | 2.16 |

*Source*: Department of Trade and Industry, *British Business*, 7 November 1986.

return on capital, which was particularly large in the manufacturing sector of the economy and also faster in the 1970s than in the earlier decades, was a fall in the share of profits in income: in the manufacturing sector this fell by a third during the 1970s. However, as part (c) of the table shows, a fall in the productivity of capital (i.e., a rise in the capital–output ratio) also contributed significantly to the decline in the profit rate. As indicated above, algebraically the capital–output ratio is determined by the ratio of capital to labour and the ratio of output to labour (i.e. the productivity of labour). Since the productivity of labour was rising in the 1960s and also in the 1970s although at a substantially slower rate (see table 1.3), it appears evident that the ratio

**Table 1.3** Productivity of labour and capital in the UK (compound annual growth rates)

|  | *1960s* | *1969–79* | *1979–82* |
|---|---|---|---|
| Labour productivity | 5.8 | 2.2 | 3.5 |
| Capital productivity | 1.1 | – 2.6 | – 4.4 |
| Total factor productivity | 4.9 | 1.1 | 1.6 |

*Source*: *OECD Economic Outlook*, May 1986, table 5, p. 10.

of capital to labour was also increasing and at a much faster rate. How far this was due to simple substitution of capital for labour, or to autonomous changes in production functions cannot easily be said. Certainly however there was a substantial fall in employment in manufacturing industry in the latter years of the 1970s, following the oil price shock of 1973–4, but a declining trend in manufacturing employment was clearly visible before this.

It is of course dangerous to draw hard and fast conclusions from the behaviour of any of these relationships without specific knowledge of underlying production functions, technical progress and so on.[26] Moreover, in the short run, profit share could be forced down and the capital–output ratio forced up by restriction on the growth of demand. But as indicated elsewhere in this book it is difficult to believe that demand deficiency (as distinct from supply side factors) was an important element in a decade in which demand in nominal money terms was increasing at an annual rate of 15 per cent. It is also difficult to believe that labour market conditions and government policy were not important. Labour markets in these years were characterized by the growth of trade union power in wage determination – a power that was increasingly buttressed by growing influence in the political scene as governments sought co-operation from unions in the search for effective incomes policies, and also by government reluctance to abandon full employment policies. The existence of a strong labour movement, determined to increase the real wages of its members and to raise income

26 A more detailed discussion of profits and employment in UK manufacturing industry, with the relevant statistical background, can be found in W.E. Martin and M. O'Connor, 'Profitability: a background paper' and G. Maynard, 'Factors affecting profitability and employment in UK Manufacturing Industry, 1960–78', chapters 2 and 6 of W.E. Martin (ed.), *The Economics of the Profits Crisis* (Dept. of Industry, HMSO, 1981).

share, and able to do so in an environment in which governments sought to maintain full employment, provides at least part of the explanation of falling profit share – and probably a major part. When accompanied by an apparent unwillingness or inability, in some industries at least, of labour and management to co-operate in making best use of new capital and technology being introduced, thereby retarding the productivity of both capital and labour, the impact on profit rate was inevitable.[27]

The role of government should not be understated; for in its anxiety to maintain full employment and growth, the government became increasingly generous in providing tax allowance incentives to investment, whilst an accommodating monetary policy kept real rates of interest low. Labour costs under the influence of strong labour unions and buoyant labour market conditions rose strongly. Thus these policies encouraged both a substitution of capital for labour within existing technology and in the longer run the introduction of more capital-using ones. More importantly, by keeping up profit net of tax it encouraged entrepreneurs to go on investing even though profit gross of tax steadily fell. Naturally this process could not continue for ever. At some point, apparently reached by large sectors of UK manufacturing industry in the early 1970s, profit fell to such low levels that tax-based investment allowances could not be taken advantage of. Profit after tax had fallen as low as profit gross of tax. Continuation of such policies then involves direct subsidization, often involving a take-over of equity or outright nationalization, with unwelcome political implications to add to the fiscal cost of subsidies in general. Even so, governments of the day, whatever their complexion, resorted to this way out.

It is obvious that a policy of subsidizing capital to promote growth and employment is subject to important constraints. An artificial lowering of the price of capital relative to the price of labour implies the need for a larger and faster growing capital stock than would otherwise be needed to absorb into employment the existing and growing labour force. Other things being equal, the investment–GDP ratio has to be higher, so that if deficits in the current balance of payments are to be avoided, the (*ex ante*) domestic saving–GDP ratio also has to be higher. Difficulties in the way of achieving the latter may mean that incipient balance of payments problems are unavoidable,[28] as a

27 Profit rates fell in most industrial countries throughout the 1960s and 1970s. Generally, however, returns to capital employed in manufacturing industry ran well above that in the UK. See *British Business*, 7 Nov. 1986.

28 An excess of domestic investment over domestic saving implies an excess of imports over exports.

consequence of which macroeconomic policy restraint may become necessary; and it becomes increasingly difficult to maintain full employment. As we have seen, employment in UK manufacturing industry fell steadily throughout the second half of the 1960s and all of the 1970s, and although increasing amounts of labour were absorbed in the service industries and especially in the public sector (the expansion of which seemed to be more motivated by employment considerations than the welfare or other needs of the public at large),[29] unemployment as a proportion of the labour force rose from less than 2 per cent in the mid 1960s to over 5 per cent at the end of the 1970s. Thus the growing balance of payments and employment difficulties experienced by the UK through the 1960s and early 1970s can be attributed fundamentally to inappropriate relative factor prices. Increasing aggregate demand to maintain full employment in the face of wrong relative factor prices (overpricing of labour, underpricing of capital) quickly pushed the country into balance of payments difficulties; and reducing that demand to correct the balance of payments led to unemployment. Trying to beat the dilemma by devaluing the exchange rate could not be successful unless labour was willing to accept a smaller share of the income generated in the manufacturing sector, either through a rise in labour productivity unmatched by an equal rise in the real wage or else by a fall in the real wage itself.

### The Oil Price Shock

The argument that the increasing unemployment and balance of payments difficulties experienced by the UK in the 1960s and the early 1970s were fundamentally due to wrong relative factor prices does not imply that the solution to them necessarily required an absolute fall in the own product real wage. As indicated above, faster rising productivity of labour, unmatched by an equally faster rise in money wages would have brought about the rise in the share of profits and rise in the rate of profit on the capital that was required. However, the problems were compounded by the steep rise in commodity, particularly oil, prices in the early 1970s. This did mean that the product real wage[30]

29 See R. Bacon and W. Eltis, *Britain's Economic Problem: Too Few Producers* (Macmillan, London, 1976) for early awareness of the problems being created for the UK economy by the relative expansion of public sector employment.

30 The product real wage is the money wage paid by the firm or industry deflated by the price of the product produced. It is not to be confused with the real wage which is the money wage deflated by the consumer price index.

would have to fall if employment in manufacturing was to be maintained. Although initially at any rate, the attention of policy makers and others was directed mainly to the demand deflationary impact of the oil price rise on the economies of the Western world – leading governments generally to follow Keynesian demand expansionary policies in the wake of the first oil price shock in 1973[31] – the more important impact exerted itself through the supply side of the industrial economies. Clearly a rise in the real price of a major product input to manufacturing industry such as oil meant a fall in net value added and claimable by labour and capital. Product real wages and returns to capital had to fall, at least until productivity could rise sufficiently to offset the need for it. Product real wages did not fall easily or quickly in the industrial world as a whole, as a consequence of which profits were squeezed and employment in manufacturing fell.

Of course, dealing with the problem posed by the massive rise in oil price was by no means easy for policy makers. Compensatory Keynesian demand expansion seemed an appropriate response to the rise in the world propensity to save, but success clearly depended on whether the higher inflation that would result would bring about a subsequent fall in the real price of oil and/or in the real wage. In fact the real price of oil did fall in the second half of the 1970s; however, the relief was short lived. Since the real demand–supply balance for oil was not affected, higher world inflation set the scene for the second oil price shock in 1979–80.[32] It is significant that the quite different policy response following this second oil price shock – monetary and fiscal squeeze instead of monetary and fiscal policy expansion – did eventually bring about a change in the oil demand and supply balance and a fall in the real price of oil.[33]

In the UK, taking the decade of the 1970s as a whole, the ratio of material (non-labour, non-capital) input prices to output prices of manufacturing industry rose by about one third, implying a fall in real

31 Although the massive public spending increase embarked on by the newly elected Labour government in 1974–5 (the public sector financial deficit increased from 3.8 % of GDP in 1973 to 7.2 per cent in 1975 – see table 5.2) was in line with its political and social philosophy, it seems clear that the government was also motivated by the conviction that a larger budget deficit was an appropriate Keynesian response to the oil price crisis.

32 A fivefold rise in the price of oil in 1973–4 was followed by a further trebling in 1979–80.

33 See G. Maynard, 'Have macroeconomic policies since 1979 been adequate to reshape OECD economies?', *Financial Markets and Economic Activities* (Financial Markets Conference, First Austrian Bank, Apr. 1983).

value added attributable to domestic labour and capital of about 20 per cent. Although, without some offsetting rise in labour productivity, a fall in the product real wage (defined as the relationship between the money wage paid in a particular firm or industry and the money price of the product of that firm or industry) was clearly required, the opposite happened; product real wages rose significantly. As a consequence, profits were further squeezed, and employment in manufacturing fell steeply.

As indicated earlier, since a relationship between own product real wages and the demand for labour did not feature in the Treasury macroeconomic model, or apparently in Treasury economic thinking at the time, UK policy makers were inclined to see the decline in employment as no more than a manifestation of a Keynesian deficiency of demand, imposed by balance of payments constraint and an overvalued exchange rate. Even as late as 1976, policy makers seemed to think that the problem could be overcome by export-led growth stimulated by a fall in the exchange rate. It would appear that an attempt was made to push down the exchange rate in early 1976, but this ended in a massive currency crisis, necessitating resort to IMF credit and conditionality at the end of the year. Although there was some attempt to keep sterling down through 1977 after confidence in the currency had returned, this was abandoned in the autumn of the year. 1976–7 probably signalled the end, at least for a time, of Treasury dreams to promote growth through an undervalued exchange rate.[34]

Despite the considerations referred to above, there are still some who explain the UK's unemployment difficulties of the 1970s in terms of demand deficiency. This seems hard to understand given that during the decade nominal final expenditure on goods and services rose fourfold (i.e. an annual rate of 15 per cent). It is of course possible to argue that even faster expansion of *nominal* demand and therefore faster inflation would have brought down the own product real wage relative to labour productivity, but the experience of many countries, particularly in Latin America, does not suggest that high inflation is an effective way of lowering the real wage. The combination of rising unemployment and balance of payments deficits despite a depreciating exchange rate suggests that the underpricing of capital and the overpricing of labour were more pertinent causes of growing unemployment.

34 Of course, the Treasury view was not monolithic at this time. No doubt some officials opposed a strategy of growth through depreciation; others saw it as the only way out.

## Keynes Discredited

It is not too much to say that events in the mid 1970s led to a total discrediting of macroeconomic policy in the UK. Of course, it can be argued that UK policy makers were singularly unfortunate in the early and mid 1970s. There was a case for introducing Competition and Credit Control in 1971; and, given the government's reliance on incomes policies, a case for introducing 'threshold' payments in 1973. Floating sterling could hardly be avoided in June 1972, given the traumas of the international monetary system. Oil price was outside the control of the British government, and an increase in government expenditure seemed an appropriate policy response. But the combination of these elements produced a lethal inflationary mixture, which duly exploded. Misfortune or not, there were fundamental faults in policy attitudes as well.

The events also led to a discrediting of Keynes and Keynes's *General Theory*, but wrongly so. Keynes in the *General Theory* did not ignore the relationship between product real wages and employment. Nor for that matter did he play down the role of monetary policy – particularly in an anti-inflationary role – as many economists have suggested he did.

Keynes defined a situation of 'involuntary unemployment' very carefully. According to him it existed when employment became fixed at a level at which the marginal product of labour (equal to the going real wage) exceeded the supply price of labour (i.e., the real wage at which that amount of labour was willingly supplied).[35] This could happen if a highly elastic demand function for money prevented the rate of interest from falling to the level at which full employment saving would be matched by investment. Given this, Keynes argued it would be appropriate for the government to increase public works expenditure even if this meant a larger budget deficit, at least temporarily. But Keynes would not have described as 'involuntary', unemployment that was due to labour demanding a *higher* price than its marginal product.[36] Nor can one really believe that Keynes would have

35 'Men are involuntarily unemployed if, in the event of a small rise in the price of wage – goods relatively to the money wage, both the aggregate supply of labour willing to work for the current money wage and the aggregate demand for it at that wage would be greater than the existing volume of employment' – Keynes, *General Theory*, p. 15.
36 Unemployment was voluntary 'due to the refusal or inability of a unit of labour, as a result of legislation or social practices or of combination for

denied that the demand for labour is a function of the relative price of labour and capital in the longer run, even though his own analysis was very short term; or that, given an open economy and possibilities of changes in the relative prices of the inputs and outputs of that economy from and to the rest of the world, the demand for labour would depend on the terms of trade as well as on the real wage. There can be little doubt that growing unemployment in the UK during the 1960s and early 1970s was much more of the voluntary (overpriced) type – arising first from a steady rise in the price of labour relatively to the price of capital, and later from a failure of the product real wage to adjust to worsening terms of trade of manufacturing industry – than of the involuntary type discussed by Keynes in the *General Theory*.

In any case, facts rather than theories began to force the abandonment of Keynesian macroeconomic policies even before the 1974–9 Labour administration of Mr Callaghan had run its course. UK economic performance in the decade of the 1970s was dismal. Between 1969 and 1979 GDP grew at barely 2 per cent per annum, not much more than two thirds of the rate of increase during the previous fifteen years. Inflation on the other hand quadrupled, averaging over 12 per cent per annum in the decade, and reaching more than 25 per cent in at least one year (1975), despite repeated attempts to reach an accord with the trade unions on an incomes policy. Total factor productivity across the economy as a whole rose at barely 1 per cent per annum whilst output and employment in manufacturing industry declined by over 12 per cent and 15 per cent respectively. Overall, unemployment rose from 2.5 per cent of the labour force to 5.5 per cent, the number of unemployed more than doubling during the decade. The current account of the balance of payments was in deficit for much of the period and sterling's exchange value fell by over 20 per cent against the US dollar and over 50 per cent against the Deutschmark. The decade finished with the country being in debt to the International Monetary Fund to the tune of £3 billion.

Of course, other countries' economic performances also deteriorated in this decade, particularly after the oil price shock of 1973; the

---

collective bargaining or a slow response to change or of mere human obstinacy, to accept a reward corresponding to the value of the product attributable to its marginal productivity' – ibid., p. 6.

Of course, in this passage and elsewhere in the *General Theory*, Keynes was assuming the existence of perfect competition in product markets. Relaxing this assumption leads to a different formulation but not to a fundamental change in the underlying thought. See chapter 6 below for a further discussion.

latter clearly had a major impact on all industrial economies. But as indicated earlier, an underlying deterioration in the UK's economic situation can be discerned well before 1973 and would have presented serious problems for policy makers even in the absence of the oil price shock. Particularly serious was the anarchic labour relations that became typical in the 1970s and which brought significant sectors of British industry, for example, the automobile industry, almost to their knees. These plagued Labour governments as well as Conservative ones and indeed were finally instrumental in bringing down Mr Callaghan's Labour government.

The trigger point was the attempt of the government to get the agreement of the trade unions to a 5 per cent pay increase for the 1978–9 pay round: only this could have ensured a return to a more reasonable inflation rate. Despite support from the more moderate trade union leaders, the attempt was defeated by a vote of the Trade Union Council (TUC) in November 1978. Less moderate leaders then put in or supported claims well in excess of 5 per cent (claims for a 30 or 40 per cent increase were not uncommon), supported in some cases (for example, the haulage and tanker drivers) by forceful secondary picketing which imposed pressure on workers and industries totally unconnected with the pay claim in dispute, or by industrial action of a very unpleasant kind (for example, the refusal of the Liverpool grave diggers to bury the dead). The combination of these excesses, and the collapse of the government's anti-inflation policy eventually precipitated a parliamentary vote of no confidence in the government; and an election followed in which the government was defeated.[37]

The unpleasant circumstances (the 'winter of discontent') surrounding the Labour government's defeat should not distract attention from the more fundamental cause. The determination of all governments in power in the 1970s, Conservative as well as Labour, to maintain full employment at almost any cost, and their attempts to get agreement on incomes policies as a means of controlling the associated inflation, put more and more power in the hands of trade union leaders who used it, understandably perhaps, to increase Labour's share in the national product and to exert influence over management. The combined impact of union aggressiveness and inappropriate Keynesian policies proved most damaging for the British economy.

37  The events leading up to the election in 1979 are described rather bitterly by Mr Callaghan in his autobiography *Time and Chance* (Collins, London, 1987).

## Long Term Decline

But it would, of course, be a mistake to attribute the plight of the British economy in 1979 solely to economic policy in the previous decade, and it is a commonly held view that the country's economic problems have historical roots going back to the Industrial Revolution itself. In his disturbing description and analysis of Britain's post-war economic decline, *The Audit of War*,[38] Corelli Barnett shows that Britain's poor post-war economic performance was already discernible in the Second World War. He dissects the problem facing the country at the beginning of that war along four, obviously overlapping, lines: geographical – the existence of acutely depressed areas, particularly in the north of the country; industrial – the existence of decayed heavy industries, like iron and steel and shipbuilding; unemployment – the existence of chronic unemployment amounting to around 20 per cent of the labour force; and finally, social – the existence of an unhealthy, ill-nourished and ill-educated working population. The war provided a cruel but temporary solution to at least some of these problems. Unemployment was absorbed by the armed forces and the armaments factories. Iron, steel, and ships could be sold regardless of cost. The aircraft, electronic, and other new industries emerged to meet the technological needs of war. Social ills could either be overlooked because of, or at least explained by, the exigencies of war (in fact, owing to US food aid and the rationing policy, large numbers of British people were better fed during the war than before it). Under conditions of wartime mobilization, Britain's productive performance appeared impressive, apparently boding well for the post-war years; but as Barnett vividly shows such optimism was based at least partly on an illusion. During the war Britain did not have to earn its living in the sense of exporting abroad to pay for vital raw materials and foodstuffs. The cost of these was covered by US aid and by loans from the Commonwealth and other sterling area countries. US lend–lease arrangements provided Britain with enormous amounts of wartime equipment, and US machines and technology equipped many British factories. Moreover, although Britain's own industrial production was substantial, maximum production was aimed at and permitted by government contracts rather than cost effectiveness. Labour relations remained poor and productivity low, even given the spur of wartime necessity.

38 Corelli Barnett, *The Audit of War* (Macmillan, London, 1986).

The end of the war introduced a new situation. US lend–lease aid was almost immediately cancelled and access to Commonwealth and Sterling Area finance ended. There was urgent need to put British industry on to a peacetime footing, so that it could earn the foreign exchange necessary to pay for imports of raw materials and foodstuffs, etc. But Britain did not possess, even at the end of the war, a modern industrial system; it had one still plagued by bad and short-sighted management, by bad industrial relations based on ideas of class conflict, and by an untrained, unskilled labour force. While some respite was provided by the virtual destruction of major trade competitors such as Germany and Japan, this could not be relied on permanently. A massive industrial reconstruction drive (an 'economic miracle') was required if Britain was to compete successfully in the post-war period. This fact was well recognized by many in Whitehall. Instead, Britain's politicians chose to create – in Corelli Barnett's graphic words – the 'New Jerusalem', for which the country possessed an inadequate real economic base. The immediate post-war government – with little or no real public opposition from the other parties – committed itself to the creation of an ambitious welfare state that would provide social security in all its forms 'from the cradle to the grave'. It committed itself to a massive housing programme which pre-empted resources that should otherwise have gone into industrial reconstruction; and it committed itself with little or no reservation and on the basis of untried Keynesian economics to maintain full employment. Part and parcel of these commitments was an endorsement of regional policies which would take work to the workers, regardless of considerations of economic productivity and efficiency.[39]

Of course none of these aims was bad in itself; indeed, given the wartime sacrifices and peacetime hopes of the British people, a move along these lines was probably politically inevitable. Nonetheless they were unrealistic given the state of the British economy. Moreover, the

39 According to Barnett (p. 247), £20 billion at 1982 prices was spent on regional policy aimed at preserving and reviving Britain's Victorian industrial regions in the north of the country (an important adjunct to full employment policy). Not only did this fail in its attempt to achieve an equal balance of employment but also it added little to Britain's productive capacity. 'These attempts were invariably made in the face of technological realities . . . and led to such futilities as bribing or compelling firms to set up new factories in industrial areas in the 1950s and 1960s, only for them to close in the 1970s and 1980s because of appalling productivity records – Courtaulds and Dunlop at Speke, Liverpool; or the Rootes car factory at Linwood near Glasgow' (Barnett, p. 256).

commitment to full employment became virtually the central objective of post-war macroeconomic policy, which had side-effects no less costly in terms of social welfare than unemployment itself. The need to secure the co-operation of the trade unions if inflationary pressures were to be contained meant legislation favourable to the unions, which effectively restricted the power of management to manage and which prevented, or at least inhibited, the introduction of improved methods of production and working practices. The adverse effects on the productivity, efficiency and long term health of the British economy were hidden for almost two decades by the lack of real competition from Britain's pre-war competitors, Germany and Japan, which faced an even larger reconstruction problem than did Britain; and also by the fact that Britain benefited from protected markets in Commonwealth and Sterling Area countries, which enabled it to sell low technology and poor quality products, creating the illusion of initial post-war export success. But, as we have seen, once Europe and Japan had fully recovered, problems began to appear in the form of chronic difficulty in combining economic growth and high employment with balance of payments equilibrium. Policy makers then began to grasp increasingly at the straw of currency devaluation in the hope of maintaining competitiveness despite inferior productivity performance and worse inflation than in its main competitor countries. However, as indicated earlier, by the 1970s, the failure of this was evident, in accelerating inflation, declining productivity growth and rising unemployment.

Corelli Barnett's damning indictment is supported by the UK's poor economic performance in the post Second World War period compared with that of its major industrial competitors. Between 1950 and 1979, the real GDP per capita of the UK rose by 2.25 per cent per annum compared with 4.75 per cent for Germany, 4 per cent for France, 4.4 per cent for Italy, 2.1 per cent for the US and 5.5 per cent for Japan.[40] Whereas in the 1950s, Britain's GDP per capita – a measure of the standard of living – had been almost top of the list of European countries, by the end of the 1970s it had fallen to sixth place, only Italy of the major industrial countries lying below it.[41] In these three decades, Britain's productivity growth both in manufacturing and across the economy as a whole lagged well behind that of its European partners, surpassing only that of the US where of course productivity was always at a much higher level. Thus, although, as we

40 Maddison, *Phases of Capitalist Development*. Estimates adjusted for overlapping periods.
41 H.M. Treasury, *Economic Progress Report*, 189 (Mar.–Apr. 1987).

# 2

# Ideology and Theory underlying the Thatcher Approach

By 1979 the British economy was in a parlous state. The previous decade had witnessed inflation rates at times touching 25 per cent and averaging more than 12 per cent. Industrial production, excluding oil and gas, was barely 4 per cent above its 1970 level and 5 per cent below its peak in 1973, whilst employment in industry had fallen by almost 9 per cent. (The de-industrialization of the UK started well before the advent of Thatcherism.) The current account of the balance of payments had been in substantial deficit for virtually the whole period, and in 1979 the UK was £3 billion in debt to the IMF and other creditors. Labour relations, particularly in the public sector, were in a state of anarchy and the incomes policy imposed by the previous administration had collapsed. Although in 1978 recorded inflation was for the first time for many years down below 10 per cent, average earnings were rising at a much faster rate, promising higher inflation in subsequent years. And, as indicated earlier, average profitability of manufacturing industry, net as well as gross of tax, had fallen to little more than 3 per cent. Substantial sections had perforce been nationalized or socialized and only survived on the basis of large government subsidies. Clearly some drastic action was required.

Strangely enough, even in 1979 there were those who broadly supported the continuation of past policies, perhaps even more so: more fiscal and monetary expansion, further depreciation of the currency, tighter incomes policies, and so on. These economists did not deny the need to reduce inflation, but because they saw little connection between aggregate expenditure on goods and services and the rate of inflation, and also believed that the decline in production and employment in the 1970s was due to a deficiency of demand, they still believed that Keynesian policies were appropriate. Despite previous experience, their faith in incomes policies remained 'touching' rather than convincing. Yet others, also taking the view that the UK's industrial problems were due to restrictive demand policies forced on the government by a balance of payments constraint, opted for import controls rather than devaluation on grounds that controls would depress real wages less than devaluation and were therefore more acceptable. The inevitable difficulties that would be posed for the UK's relationships with its EEC and other trading partners were perhaps glossed over.

Although in some respects the policies to be pursued by the new government had been foreshadowed in measures forced on the previous government by the crisis facing them – for example, monetary targeting and restrictions on government spending and borrowing – it can still be said that Mrs Thatcher's policies provided a complete break with the past.[1] Inevitably it invited the opposition of much, although by no means all, of the economics profession.

## Monetarism

The new strategy effectively abandoned Keynesian short run demand management aimed at full or high employment. Instead, emphasis was placed on improving the long run supply side performance of the economy. Deregulation, the abandonment of controls over prices, incomes and capital movements; the return of state-owned industries to private ownership and management; and, as urgent as anything, reduction in the power of trade unions and reform of labour laws, were all seen to be necessary. An urgent priority was to reduce inflation and to establish an environment of price stability, since without this the supply side performance of the economy could not be improved. The proposed method of doing this was by monetary control, incomes policy being rejected partly on grounds of its demonstrable ineffectiveness and partly because control over incomes was incompatible with improved supply side performance. With the abandonment of short run demand management, fiscal policy became a matter of reducing

1 As indicated in ch. 1 (fn. 2), the previous Conservative administration under Mr Heath had started out with the intention of bringing about a significant change in policy but was soon forced into a U-turn. There can be little doubt that Mrs Thatcher, as a minister in that administration, learned much from that experience, in particular, the danger attached to U-turns.

both government expenditure and taxation relatively to GDP, as a means of increasing incentives and resources for the private sector. Although it was clearly unrealistic to think of balancing the fiscal budget in any quick period of time, this seemed to constitute a long term aim.

Undoubtedly much ideology underlay the Thatcher approach. Mrs Thatcher was quickly identified as a believer in hard work, family responsibility and duty to one's country; the Victorian virtues of self-help and balancing one's income and expenditure, and Adam Smith's teaching of the virtues of free markets and the inefficiencies of government intervention were made much of. But the downplaying of fiscal policy and the greater emphasis on monetary policy appeared to be influenced also by developments in economic theory and knowledge in the previous two decades.

As described in the previous chapter, fiscal policy – the manipulation of government expenditure and taxation and the balance between them – had been the centre-piece of macroeconomic policy in the UK for most of the post-war period: monetary policy played a very subordinate role, largely, although not wholly, because for most of these years the UK maintained a fixed exchange rate. In so far as monetary policy was employed, it took the form of controls on bank lending and hire purchase, i.e. control over credit, rather than control over the quantity of money *per se*. Although not in favour of control over bank lending except in extraordinary circumstances, the Radcliffe Report of 1959, with its emphasis on 'liquidity' and the structure of interest rates rather than on money supply, provided the intellectual rationale of this approach.[2] But not all economists were convinced of the ineffectiveness of monetary policy, and not all were convinced that fiscal policy had quite the potent impact on aggregate demand that Keynesian economics affirmed. Indeed, even prior to the Thatcher administration, governments were being forced by academic pressure and even more by the course of events to give greater attention to control over money supply; and, as indicated earlier, explicit monetary targets were in fact set by the Labour government in 1976. However, no explicit linkage to the fiscal deficit was introduced at this time.

It seems unlikely that the new Conservative government of 1979 was converted to 'monetarism' simply by econometric evidence provided

---

2 The Committee on the working of the Monetary System, chaired by Lord Radcliffe played down the role of money in the economic and financial system, giving pride of place to 'liquidity', which, however, was not clearly defined and certainly not measurable.

by sections of the academic profession, although no doubt some of the key researchers and proselytizers of the doctrine (e.g. Professor Milton Friedman and Professor Alan Walters) were very influential. More likely it was influenced by the rather common-sense and long-held notion that printing money in excess would eventually affect prices ('too much money chasing too few goods') and that, in order to stop inflation, governments had to restrict the quantity of money.

However, if policy makers are to rely on control over money supply as a practical matter, then certain conditions have to be satisfied. First, money must have an identifiable form, which remains relatively stable through time (what serves as money today must serve as money tomorrow). Second, money supply must be stably and predictably related, directly or indirectly, to the variable the government wishes to influence; and third, the government must have a reliable means of exercising control over it.

By definition, money is that commodity which is immediately exchangeable into goods and services and other assets. In a modern economy, such as the UK, it takes the form of banknotes and coin issued by government agencies and quasi-agencies, such as a Central Bank, and chequable deposits at commercial banks. But households and firms typically hold more monetary type claims on commercial banks than they require for day-to-day transactions; and this 'surplus to transactions' type money may be held in non chequable accounts which carry interest. These quasi-money assets have an advantage over other types of interest-bearing financial assets, such as bonds, in being very easily and quickly converted into transaction money without risk of loss of value in terms of money itself. Central banks usually distinguish between *narrow* money, i.e. money immediately available for transactions but not (until recently) carrying interest, and *wider* money, which includes other interest-bearing and capital-safe claims on commercial banks in addition to narrow money. As we shall see, the distinction has become increasingly blurred, giving rise to problems discussed in later chapters.

As far as the second condition mentioned earlier is concerned, if the object is to control inflation then whether narrow money is targeted or wide money is targeted depends on which, if either, has the closest relationship with the price level. In fact, monetarists recognize that, except perhaps in the long run, neither narrow nor wide money is closely related to the price level, and that the focus of attention must be the relationship between the chosen money supply and the flow of nominal national income and expenditure, i.e. money GDP. The Radcliffe Committee's view was that no stable relationship existed between money supply, however defined, and money GDP, giving rise to the conclusion (not wholly embraced by the Radcliffe Committee itself) that if that was the case, government influence over money GDP was best exercised through controls over bank lending. Subsequent research in the 1960s began to cast doubt on the Radcliffe conclusion, and suggested that despite short run – quarter on quarter, even year on year – instability, a *long run* stable relationship did exist between a wide concept of money supply (Sterling M3)[3] and money GDP, in which, however, the rate of interest also entered.[4]

The fact that the demand for money bears some relationship to both money GDP and the rate of interest should perhaps surprise no one. The greater the value of monetary transactions being undertaken (i.e. the greater the money GDP), the larger is the amount of money required for transaction purposes; on the other hand, the higher the interest rate paid on financial assets other than money, the greater the incentive to economize on money balances held. Thus a relationship of the kind indicated in figure 2.1 – in which the ratio of money to money GDP is inversely related to the rate of interest – could reasonably be expected. What impressed monetarists however was the apparent *stability* of the relationship over a long period of time. In most years, the point connecting the rate of interest with the ratio of money to money GDP falls on or close to the line drawn.

Admittedly there were years when the relationship departed significantly from its long term form. In the early 1970s, when money supply exploded and its ratio to money GDP rose sharply, interest rates were much lower than the long term relationship would indicate; but the aberration could be explained partly by government moves to abolish direct quantitative and qualitative control over bank lending with the aim of bringing about a more competitive financial system (Competition and Credit Control), the impact of which could be expected to be temporary, and partly by the reluctance of the government to see short term interest rates rise at a time when it had embarked on a massive fiscal expansion. Subsequent years showed a return to the earlier relationship, and the faith of monetarists was restored. Thus, although the chain of causation was perhaps not clear, there seemed sufficient evidence in 1979 to support the view that, in the long run at any rate, growth of spending and nominal incomes was restrained by money supply. However as we shall see in chapters 4 and 5, the relationship

3  See ch. 1, fn. 22.
4  M. Artis and M.K. Lewis, 'How stable is the demand for money in the UK?', *Economica* (Nov. 1984).

failed to hold in the 1980s, causing problems for the new government's monetary policy.

The apparent stability of the relationship between Sterling M3 and money GDP was convenient as far as the third condition specified for effective monetary targeting is concerned. Sterling M3 corresponds very largely to the total deposit liabilities of the banking system and is therefore broadly matched by bank lending, to both public and private sectors of the economy. Changes in interest rates can be expected to affect both the willingness of bank customers to hold bank deposits and their willingness or ability to borrow from banks. Thus a rise in interest rates on alternative financial assets such as bonds could be expected to lead depositors to switch out of deposits into bonds; at the same time, if reflected in higher interest rates on bank lending, it would discourage other customers from borrowing from banks. Thus interest rates appeared to provide an effective means of controlling Sterling M3.[5] Moreover, since the public sector was an important borrower from the banks, emphasis on Sterling M3 seemed to bring out in a fairly transparent manner the relationship between monetary expansion and fiscal policy: *cet. par.*, less government borrowing would mean less money creation. Unfortunately, as we shall see later, control over Sterling M3 proved less easy than was thought.

## Fiscal Policy

Turning to fiscal policy, the Thatcher government was undoubtedly influenced by the seen need to get both taxation and expenditure down; certainly they were unimpressed by the case for regulating government expenditure and the size of the budget deficit as a means of creating employment or regulating aggregate demand. Here again they had some support from non-Keynesian economists, but here also this support was unlikely to have been crucial for determining the shift in fiscal policy. According to some, Mrs Thatcher's instincts as a prudent housewife were more important!

The simple Keynesian view on fiscal policy was that government expenditure increased aggregate demand whilst taxation reduced it, the net effect being amplified by multiplier effects. Thus if unemployed resources existed, then government expenditure should be increased or

5 Narrow money, on the other hand, being largely held for transaction purposes, would be related more to nominal money income and expenditure than to interest rates.

)n reduced so as to increase aggregate demand, to the extent ary to restore full employment. The impact on total national ᴄₓₚₑₙditure and output (i.e. money GDP) would not necessarily be confined to the increase in government expenditure (or cut in taxes) itself since incomes would be created in the private sector, leading to a secondary increase in spending. In the language of the economist, there would be multiplier effects. The size of the 'multiplier', i.e. the relationship between the total increase in expenditure and output on the one hand and the initial or primary increase in government spending or cut in taxes on the other, would depend on the propensity to spend of the private sector, allowing for leakages such as increased tax payments based on the incremental income of the private sector (i.e. there would be a reverse tax flow), increased private sector saving, and also spending on imported goods rather than domestically produced ones. On the basis of realistic values of tax, saving and import propensities, a multiplier greatly in excess of 1 was commonly expected. Financing the budget deficit was not seen as a problem: either on the basis of increased private sector saving the government could sell more bonds, or, in the last resort, if unemployed resources existed, money could be created without fear of inflation. Of course in practice the approach was more sophisticated than this, but there was a general belief in the power of fiscal policy.

Early debate centred on the question whether fiscal expansion unsupported by monetary expansion could be effective. Leaving aside the mechanics of financing a possible budget deficit, the simple monetarist view based on the assumption of a broadly constant ratio of money to money GDP, (i.e. a constant velocity of circulation of money) was that money GDP could not increase unless money were created: in the absence of money creation, the need to issue government bonds to finance fiscal expansion would force up interest rates sufficiently to cut private sector demand proportionately. On the other hand, if money were created, expansion would follow without a fiscal expansion being necessary. Moreover, on the assumption that full employment was the general rule, prices rather than output would rise.

Of course, few monetarists believed then or presumably believe now that the economy is permanently in a state of full employment; and few would deny that there is some interest rate elasticity in the demand for money, so that a fiscally induced expansion with rising interest rates is possible without (or at least with a less than proportionate accommodating) increase in money supply (see figure 2.1). But most would adopt the position that if unemployed resources exist, this is less due to a shortage of demand that could be corrected by Keynesian expansion, whether monetary or fiscal based, than due to supply side factors such as too high a real wage; and most would also adopt the position that private sector demand, both consumption and investment, are rather interest rate elastic so that even a small rise in interest rates necessary to permit money GDP to rise relatively to the money stock would quickly 'crowd-out' private sector demand.

Some economists also put weight on the possibility of 'direct' crowding out – as distinct from the 'financial crowding-out' referred to above – and 'confidence' effects. Direct crowding-out occurs if government provision of certain services – for example, education or health – simply replaces private provision of the same services. If the replacement is one to one then clearly an increase in government expenditure directed at increasing the supply of such services has no real expansionary impact on the economy. (It may indeed have a real contractionary effect if public sector provision is less efficient than private sector provision.) However, given that the government is a *de facto* and usually a *de jure* monopolist in the supply of such goods or services, direct crowding out is probably small and certainly less than 100 per cent.

Government spending may also influence private spending in both negative and positive directions through 'confidence' effects. Thus if the private sector has confidence in the government's ability to maintain high employment and increase growth through higher public sector spending, its own spending may be positively affected, providing further stimulus to employment and growth. At other times, however, if increased public spending leads to expectations of increased taxation or rationing or higher interest rates, private spending may fall, even before higher taxes or interest rates take effect. Professor Walters has suggested that the size of the budget deficit may be an important determinant of confidence effects: an increase in government spending when the budget deficit is negligible, possibly even negative, will have no depressing confidence effects; but the same increase in expenditure when the budget deficit is already large gives rise to fears about future taxes and interest rates and may result in no increase in total expenditure, perhaps even in net terms to a fall. Conversely, a cut in the budget deficit could actually increase total spending and output.[6]

Although post-war macroeconomic policy was based heavily on the belief that fiscal expansion (increased government expenditure and/or reduced taxation) was an effective way of increasing real output and

6 See A. Walters, *Britain's Economic Renaissance* (Oxford University Press, 1986), pp. 27–32.

employment, the empirical evidence is less than reassuring. In theory, fiscal expansion should have a greater impact on real output and employment when unemployment exists than when the labour force is fully employed: in the latter case, we would expect prices rather than output to be affected most. (In the jargon of economics, the nominal multiplier would be greater than the real multiplier.) In fact, these expectations are by no means fully borne out. A reassessment of the inter-war years 1929–37, when unemployment was very high, has shown that a strong output recovery in 1931–7 was associated with contractionary rather than expansionary fiscal policy: expansionary monetary policy appeared more significant.[7] Even if other items of autonomous expenditure – gross capital formation and exports – are included with government expenditure in the primary spending injection, real multipliers in the period 1922–39 have been shown to be very low although nominal money multipliers were expectedly high. More pertinently from our point of view, real multipliers in the post Second World War period appear to have been higher in the 1950s and 1960s, when unemployment was very low, than in the 1970s, when unemployment was higher and rising.[8]

Nevertheless, there is probably general agreement among economists that fiscal policy as exercised through government expenditure and taxation and the balance between them did have a net expansionary impact on the economy in the 1950s and 1960s, and real multipliers were significantly positive. There are obvious difficulties in the way of measuring the net primary impact of expenditure and taxation on the economy – in the sense of estimating what would be the impact on GDP if, say, both expenditure and taxation were reduced to zero – even if direct and indirect crowding out and confidence effects could be ignored. The real demand impact on the economy of government expenditure clearly depends on the distribution between expenditure on goods and services and that on transfer payments; also in the case of the demand reducing impact of taxation, on the relative shares of direct and indirect taxation in the total. (The propensity to consume of the typical transfer payment – e.g. pension – recipient differs from that of the typical taxpayer.) One attempt to estimate the net primary impact

7 See P. Sedgwick, 'Economic recovery in the 1930s', *Bank of England Paper*, 2, (Apr. 1984). See also H. Rose, 'Another look at the inter-war period', *Barclay's*, *Review*, 58/1 (Feb. 1983), which also stresses the importance of monetary policy *vis-à-vis* fiscal policy.

8 See *Britain's Economic Renaissance*, ch. Walters, ch 1 for a fuller discussion of pre- and post-war multipliers.

of government fiscal operations on the British economy in the 1950s and 1960s suggested that it lay between 4 and 6 per cent of GDP, with a short term nominal multiplier of 2½ and a real multiplier of somewhat less than 2.[9]

The 1950s and 1960s were undoubtedly a period of relative stability and policy consensus (Butskellism) in the UK,[10] although, as indicated in chapter 1, problems in industry were beginning to arise. Moreover the budget deficit averaged less than 3½ per cent of GDP, rising above 4 per cent only towards the end. 'Confidence' in the Walters sense, might therefore seem to have existed. The 1970s of course were quite different. Stability was shattered, first by the breakdown of the Bretton Woods international monetary system and the move to floating exchange rates, and second by the oil price shock of 1973–4. Monetary policy became reckless and in the attempt to stave off rising unemployment and recession, governments resorted to larger and larger fiscal expansion. Public spending which had approximated to 33 per cent of GDP in 1960 and 37.6 per cent in 1970 shot up to 45 per cent in 1975. The budget deficit got larger and larger, and by 1975/6 amounted to over 7 per cent of GDP, twice the average for the 1950s and 1960s.[11] GDP growth and employment however did not benefit, both declining as compared with the earlier period. Estimated (*ex post*) real multipliers were much smaller than in the 1960s; and even in the mid 1980s when unemployment was even higher, most estimates put the value at well below 1.[12] Of course the problem did not lie on the side of demand, although governments behaved as though it did by pumping more of it in: higher inflation rather than increased output was the result. As indicated in chapter 1, the problem lay on the supply side of the economy, in particular in excessive real wage growth at the expense of return on capital, exacerbated by the failure of the real wage to adjust to the oil price increase and worsening terms of trade. In the jargon of the economist, the movement to the right in the aggregate

9 G. Maynard and W. van Ryckeghem, *A World of Inflation* (Batsford, London, 1976), ch. 6.

10 The post-war consensus on policy between the political parties was labelled as 'Butskellism' after Mr Butler and Mr Gaitskell, leading proponents of the policy in Conservative and Labour governments respectively, but in view of the events of the 1970s, an injustice may have been done to both of them.

11 See ch. 5, table 5.2.

12 See Walters, *Britain's Economic Renaissance*, ch. 3 for a review of the evidence.

demand curve was accompanied by an even larger move in the aggregate supply curve in the same direction, as a result of worsening terms of trade and money wage explosion as the labour force attempted to maintain an untenable real wage. The fact that the problem was misspecified did not prevent Keynesian policies from taking the blame.

## The Medium Term Financial Strategy

Thus a combination of ideology, intellectual conviction (although of course not unopposed) and the rather disastrous macroeconomic experience of the 1970s produced a radical shift in the UK macroeconomic policy: abandonment of demand management and downplaying of fiscal policy, in favour of emphasis on monetary control aimed at the elimination of inflation. This shift to 'monetarism', as the new policy was soon described, was enshrined in the adoption of a medium term financial strategy (MTFS) embracing both fiscal and monetary policy. The objective of the MTFS was a progressive reduction in the rate of inflation, and its instruments were declining targets for monetary growth and budgetary deficits over an initial period of four years. These are described in chapter 4, which deals with the implementation of the strategy from 1979 to 1987.

Although 'monetarism' is in principle quite independent of fiscal policy, linking the two together in a financial strategy appeared to the new government to make sense, since it provided a basis for monetary restriction and declining inflation to go hand in hand with falling nominal and real interest rates, so providing a stimulus to private sector demand.[13] Perhaps equally important, however, was the feeling that monetary policy and monetary targeting would appear more credible, and thus have a greater effect on inflationary expectations, if government was seen to be reducing its own demand for credit. Declining inflationary expectations would in turn make it more likely that monetary restriction would pull down inflation with little effect on output and employment.

It is noteworthy that PSBR (public sector borrowing requirement) targets were set without explicit reference to the cyclical state of the economy – i.e., the relationship between actual output and full employment capacity output – and drew criticism from many economists on that score (see chapter 5). It had been broadly accepted by

13 How far this is true in a world in which capital is internationally mobile will be discussed in ch. 5.

macroeconomists that, other things being equal, budget deficits would tend to be larger when the economy was in recession than when it was operating at full employment (tax revenue would be cyclically lower and some items of government expenditure, e.g. unemployment pay, would be cyclically higher), and that governments should not attempt to offset this by raising taxes generally or reducing other items of government expenditure since this would make the recession worse.

That no attempt was made to split the targeted PSBRs into cyclical and structural components can be defended on grounds that the new government wished to make it very clear that its medium term aim was to bring about a better balance between expenditure and tax revenue – an aim that would certainly have been obscured if in practice PSBRs had shown a tendency to rise over time rather than fall, particularly in the early years of the strategy. Moreover, whether cyclically adjusted or simply structural, deficits have to be financed and therefore have an impact on financial markets which feed through to the private sector. Rapidly growing public sector deficits through the 1970s – justified on grounds that growing unemployment required demand expansionary measures – clearly contributed to financial deterioration and high inflation, with adverse effects on private sector activity and the overall performance of the British economy. No government whatever its political colour – least of all one with the aims of the new government – could have continued with such macro policies, whatever theoretical economists might say. In practice, as we shall see in chapter 4, the new government did not stick rigidly to its initially announced targets, and actual PSBRs exceeded those targets in subsequent years. Nonetheless, the objective of declining PSBRs relative to GDP was achieved and in this sense the MTFS strategy was maintained.


### Employment Policy


Abandonment of short run demand management, and the priority to be given to reducing inflation, seemed to leave the new government without an explicit policy for employment. There was perhaps a temptation on its part to accept a somewhat extreme version of the monetarist doctrine that suggested that because of 'rational expectations', money stock changes would feed rapidly into price changes and later in money wage settlements, with output and employment only temporarily, if at all, affected[14] – a view however which was probably

14 According to the doctrine of 'rational expectations' transactors can be

not held by the most influential of the government's supporters and teachers. More likely the government was persuaded by arguments, current among economists at the time, that although a reduction in inflation necessitated some rise in unemployment, this would be only temporary. Once inflation had reached the desired level, employment would rise again. Behind the line of argument lay a belief in the existence of a level of unemployment at which inflation would be stable – i.e., the non-accelerating inflation rate level of unemployment (the NAIRU). Unemployment above this level would push inflation down; unemployment below it would push inflation up. Implicitly this belief contained a further belief in the equilibratory nature of the labour market: declining demand for labour relatively to supply would lower the rate of increase in money wages, thus sustaining inflation at its new lower level, without a permanent rise in the unemployment level being necessary.[15]

Whether or not the concept of the NAIRU underpinned the new government's views on the relationship between inflation and unemployment, the government certainly subscribed to the view that the labour market had to be made more competitive – i.e., more likely to produce the flexibility in the money and real wage that was necessary to restore and maintain full employment. Hence it had in mind legislation that would reduce the monopoly power of the trade unions in wage bargaining. Such ideas fitted in with its general intention to curb the power of trade unions more widely, to reduce restrictive practices, and to lessen the influence of the unions over economic policy making. The legislation that flowed from this intention will be described in chapter 4.

Trade union reform was of course seen as a major contribution to improved supply side performance of the British economy, and no doubt had the support of a substantial proportion of the British

---

expected to take into account all information available to them – both past and expected future – when taking decisions, and to have in mind an analytical model which they believe explains how the economy works. Thus, according to 'rational expectationists', wage bargainers will infer from the imposition of monetary targets that future inflation will fall, hence they will demand lower wage settlements. See D.K. Begg, *The Rational Expectations Revolution in Macroeconomics* (Philip Allan, Deedington, 1982).

15 The NAIRU should not be confused with the Phillips curve. Whereas the latter relates the level of unemployment to the change in money wages (and therefore – given an assumption about productivity – the rate of inflation), the former relates the unemployment level to the *change* in the inflation rate.

electorate, including many in the trade union movement itself. Other measures, including proposals to return to private ownership state-owned industries (privatization) and the abolition of controls over incomes, prices and capital movements were also seen as important but may have had less support from the electorate in general.

The government was also committed to raising work and saving incentives through structural reform in the tax system and cuts in the burden of tax, but the scale at which changes were introduced in its first budget surprised many of its own supporters, let alone opponents, and it had macro effects that were probably not fully expected (see chapter 4).

In brief, the policies aimed at by Mrs Thatcher's first administration represented a substantial change from those pursued in the post-war period. Although elements of the new policies had seen the light of day in earlier administrations – for example, monetary targeting intro-duced by the Labour government in April 1976 – the whole repre-sented more than the sum of the parts. In rejecting Keynesian short run demand management, the new approach seemed to represent a return to classical macroeconomics prior to Keynes: ideas of balanced bud-gets, of the quantity theory of money, of equilibrating labour markets, of supply determining demand rather than demand determining supply, returned to the centre of the stage. Naturally it didn't work out quite like this, as later chapters in this book will show; but nonetheless, as will be argued later, there was a significant change of philosophy which might be summarized as the substitution of an attitude of 'non-accommodation' of wage and other price-raising pressures for an atti-tude of 'accommodation' to them. Critics of the change in attitude saw it of course as the replacement of 'conciliation' with 'confrontation'. Few can deny however that the change has had a significant impact on the performance of the British economy.

However, it is necessary to note that the introduction of the new strategy coincided with an enforced structural change of the UK economy associated with the country becoming a significant oil pro-ducer. Clearly the transition from being a net importer of oil to a net exporter at a time of a substantial rise in the price of oil was of consider-able benefit to the UK; but it also created problems. The impact of the new economic strategy could not be unaffected by the change in the UK's energy status or indeed by the impact of the rise in oil price on the rest of the world. Hence, before examining the implementation of the strategy and its results, it is convenient to examine the opportunities and problems created by North Sea oil.

# 3

# Opportunities and Problems posed by North Sea Oil

## Production and Price Background

Although exploration for oil in the UK sector of the North Sea began in the mid 1960s, production did not start on a significant scale until 1975. Thereafter, oil production rose rapidly so that by 1980 the UK had become self-sufficient, and in 1981 it became a net exporter (see table 3.1). Production probably peaked in the mid 1980s (at around 130 million tonnes a year) and will fall to about 80–90 million tonnes in 1990. Beyond 1990, there is a great deal of uncertainty – since, apart from geological uncertainties, exploration and development are sensitive to net oil prices, technology and of course government depletion policy – but for our purposes, the Department of Energy's forecast of oil production through to the year 2020 will be accepted, as will Shell UK's forecast of oil demand over the same period. These forecasts suggest that UK self-sufficiency will remain until about the year 2000. Thereafter oil production will fall rather rapidly, and by year 2020 the UK will once again be largely dependent on imports for its oil supply.

Several questions arise concerning the impact of North Sea oil on the British economy. How far was Britain made better off by having North Sea oil? What was the effect on Britain's comparative position *vis-à-vis* other major industrial countries? And what, if any, were the unavoidable effects on Britain's tradable sector, in particular, manufacturing industry?

In approaching these questions we should note that the rise of the UK as an oil producer broadly coincided with the massive rise in oil price that began in the early 1970s and ended, at least temporarily, in

**Table 3.1** UK oil production and consumption, 1973–2020 (millions tonnes)

|  | Production[a] | Consumption[b] |
|---|---|---|
| 1973 | 0.4 | 113.7 |
| 1974 | 0.4 | 106.4 |
| 1975 | 1.6 | 93.3 |
| 1976 | 12.2 | 92.5 |
| 1977 | 38.3 | 92.8 |
| 1978 | 54.0 | 94.0 |
| 1979 | 77.9 | 94.0 |
| 1980 | 80.5 | 80.8 |
| 1981 | 88.0 | 74.8 |
| 1982 | 100.4 | 75.5 |
| 1983 | 111.0 | 72.4 |
| 1984 | 121.0 | 89.6 |
| 1985 | 122.0 | 77.8 |
| *Estimated* | | |
| 1990 | 80–90 | 70.0 |
| 2000 | 50–90 | 72.5 |
| 2010 | 30–70 | 72.5 |
| 2020 | 10–25 | 72.5 |

[a] Including condensates, ethane, propane and butane.
[b] Energy products, non-energy products, refinery fuel and losses, and marine bunkers.
*Source*: C. Robinson and E. Marshall *Oil's Contribution to UK Self-Sufficiency* (Heinemann Educational Books, London, 1984).

1981. Although by virtue of becoming an oil producer in the second half of the 1970s, the UK was placed in a more favourable position than other major industrial countries, it was by no means shielded completely from the impact of the price rise. Oil price quadrupled in 1973–4 before UK oil production began at all, so that in these years and the immediate following ones until production began in 1976, the UK was no better off than other importers, except perhaps in so far as the UK was more easily able to borrow in international capital markets to cover the initial resource cost. As oil production rose, the *relative* position of the UK improved as compared with other major oil importers. Even so, the UK could not avoid the real burden of the oil price rise since real resources had to be devoted to domestic production of oil. Although the cost of production of UK oil did not rise to the level of the oil price on world markets, it was still higher than the cost of imported oil before its price rose in 1973 (pre-1973–4 imported oil cost about £23 per tonne in 1980 prices whereas the real resource cost of UK-produced oil amounted to about £35–40 per tonne, again in 1980 prices).[1] Thus, *far from the UK enjoying an oil bonanza in the second half of the 1970s, in absolute terms the UK was actually worse off than in 1972.*

However, the real resource cost of North Sea oil was well below the post-1973 import price, so that as the *share* of domestic oil production in British consumption rose in the second half of the 1970s, the average real cost of oil to the UK fell as compared with 1973–4; as a consequence, by 1979–80, when the second oil price shock occurred, the UK was obtaining its oil at roughly half the real cost facing other importers. Being self-sufficient in oil, the UK was shielded from the more than doubling of real oil price that took place through 1979–80. When production began to exceed consumption in 1981 and the following years, the UK becoming a net exporter, the country began to recuperate (at oil importers' expense) some of the absolute loss it had suffered in the 1970s. In 1981–2, the real resource cost of oil to the UK was barely a third of the cost it would have had to pay without North Sea oil. Since in the years 1981–3, UK net exports of oil amounted to about one third of oil production, the net gain to the UK was substantial.

Throughout the period, the UK charged domestic consumers of oil the world price, and the rent obtained by the UK from North Sea oil production accrued in the form of substantial tax revenue. This enabled government expenditure to be higher or taxes and government domestic borrowing to be lower than would otherwise have been the case, with further effects on the economy that were important.

## Macroeconomic Effects in Principle and Practice[2]

A country which moves from being a substantial net importer of oil to being self-sufficient is clearly likely to experience significant

1 *Bank of England Quarterly Bulletin* (London, Mar. 1982), chart 5, North Sea Oil and Gas.

2 The literature on the impact of North Sea oil on the UK economy is becoming too extensive to be cited here. The brief analytical discussion introducing this section has been influenced most by two articles by P.J. Forsyth and J.A. Kay: 'The economic implications of North Sea oil revenue' and 'Oil revenues and manufacturing output' appearing in *Fiscal Studies*, 1/3 (July 1980) and 2/2 (July 1981) respectively, and one by W.M. Corden: 'The exchange rate, monetary policy and North Sea oil', *Oxford Economic Papers*, 30, July Supplement.

macroeconomic effects. It may be useful to consider these in principle before turning to the case of the UK.

If the achievement of self-sufficiency involves the use of domestic real resources which otherwise would have gone into exports to pay for imported oil, these effects will take the form of shifts between domestic industries and may not be very significant. The matter is different if a rise in oil sufficiency involves an increment of income over and above the opportunity cost of resources used in oil production, i.e. economic rent, since now the economy can be better off and real aggregate demand can be expanded.

Ignoring the transition to self-sufficiency, i.e. assuming in effect that the economy becomes self-sufficient overnight, this increment of income will initially take the form of an improvement in the country's balance of trade with the rest of the world. At minimum, real aggregate demand can be expanded to absorb this improvement; but if the economy has unemployed resources the use of which has been constrained by the balance of payments (i.e. inability to sell more exports and thus earn more export revenue or to reduce the ratio of imports to expenditure), real aggregate demand can be expanded by a multiple of the increment of income. This multiple depends on the ratio of imports to total demand at the margin (i.e. on the marginal propensity to import). Gross domestic product therefore rises as well as non-oil imports. However, the *composition* of gross domestic production must usually change since the increment of income is likely to produce an increase in the demand for non-tradables (i.e. goods and services which do not enter into international trade) as well as tradables, whereas the initial increment of supply (i.e. rise in non-oil imports or fall in exports) will take the form of tradables. Thus whatever happens to the output of tradables (largely manufactures) which need not necessarily fall, the share of these in GDP will fall while the share of non-tradables will rise.

However, in the case of industrial countries, what appears to be a balance of payments constraint is more often than not a real domestic resource constraint even when unemployed resources appear to exist. The most likely cause of this constraint is an unwillingness of the labour force to accept a real wage at which full employment, conventionally defined, can be achieved. (If this were not the case, a depreciation of the exchange rate would eliminate the balance of payments constraint.) Given a *full employment* assumption or an equivalent domestic supply constraint, not only will the share of tradables in GDP fall when oil-related income arises, but so also will the absolute volume of output of these goods. Productive resources are shifted towards non-tradables in response to the rise in demand. Unemployment can of course result if labour is neither mobile nor prepared to accept the change in relative real wages that might be required by a shift of labour from tradables to non-tradables. The mechanism that brings about this shift in resources is a rise in the *real* exchange rate, induced either by an appreciation of the nominal exchange rate or by a rise in the domestic price level relative to that abroad. Which of these eventualities occurs depends on the stance of domestic monetary policy.

All of these effects could be avoided if the newly oil sufficient country invested the whole of its newly created economic rent abroad – although offsetting capital inflows may make this policy option unfeasible – but such a policy means that benefits from oil resources, in terms of domestic consumable incomes, are forgone or at any rate postponed. In general, of course, the precise impact of a country becoming an oil producer depends on the nature of other policies being pursued.

Similar macroeconomic effects – a shift towards non-tradables – can be expected in an oil sufficient economy as a result of a rise in the world price of oil. Although the oil sufficient country is insulated in resource terms from such a rise, its real exchange rate will tend to appreciate either because of the downward pressure on the exchange rates of net oil importing countries which have to increase their net exports of tradables to pay for higher priced oil, and/or because of the emergence of capital inflows originating in surplus oil producing countries looking for profitable or safer assets. Here again the share of tradables in GDP and possibly the output of the oil sufficient country will be affected.

Applying the foregoing analysis to the UK, it is convenient to divide the period 1973–85 into three phases, although clearly the demarcation lines are a little blurred. In the first phase, 1973–6, the UK suffered the full impact of the quadrupling of oil price, affecting all importing countries, since its oil production was negligible. In the second phase, 1976–80, during which, despite year to year fluctuations, the real oil price was roughly stabilized at its 1974 level, the UK remained dependent on imports, although to a declining extent as domestic oil production rose. In the third phase, 1980–6, the UK became self-sufficient in, and soon a net exporter of, oil at a time when the real price of oil again rose substantially. Thus we can consider separately (as well, of course, as assess the combined impact through the period as a whole) first, the impact of a price rise on an industrialized fully dependent oil-importing country; second, the effect of a rise in domestic production in that economy and a decline in its import dependency, the real price of oil being assumed constant; and third, the consequence of a rise in oil price for such an economy which has now emerged as both self-sufficient and, very soon after, a significant exporter.

In the first phase, of course, there was pressure on the UK, as on all other industrial oil-importing countries, to devote more of its domestic resources and output to the purchase of imported oil, so that the *share* of tradables, very largely manufactures, in GDP as well as tradables output in absolute terms could *ceteris paribus* be expected to rise. (In the jargon now commonly used, the UK had to 'industrialize'). Of course, a shift of resources away from non-tradables to tradables, even in a relative sense, takes time, so that in the short period comprising phase one for the UK (three to four years), such a shift would not necessarily show up in the statistics. More important, the need for resource shift was reduced since, like many other oil-importing countries, the UK resorted to external borrowing and running down of its external foreign exchange reserves to meet the extra cost of imported oil. Public sector foreign borrowing plus use of foreign exchange reserves met about half of the £3 billion increase in the UK's oil import bill from 1973 to 1976.[3] However, despite the apparent need of the UK to 'industrialize', the share of manufacturing in GDP fell during these years, as did the volume of manufacturing output. Clearly the world recession of 1975 had something to do with this.

In the next phase (1976–80), because of a fall in the *average* cost of oil to the UK from its 1973–4 level (resulting from the progressive substitution of North Sea oil for imported oil), the pressure on the UK to devote manufacturing resources to obtain oil – imported plus domestic production – declined *as compared with 1973–4, assuming that in these years the UK had in fact shifted real resources to pay for imported oil rather than resort to external borrowing.* As compared with 1972, however, the UK could not have got by with a smaller manufacturing sector either in absolute terms or related to its GDP if it was to obtain the same quantity of oil as then, even though some of the resources required to produce North Sea oil were borrowed from abroad in the form of capital inflow. Foreign inflows roughly covered the import content of the operating, development and exploration costs of North Sea oil, and these represented about half of expenditures in the mid 1970s, falling to about 15 per cent in 1980.[4] Against this, interest and dividends have to be paid on the foreign capital, imposing a future claim on the UK's own production of tradables.

3 *UK Balance of Payments 1984*, table 10.1 (Central Statistical Office).
4 *Bank of England Quarterly Bulletin* (Mar. 1982), North Sea Oil and Gas, table B and accompanying text.

Taking the 1970s as a whole, there was no need *in principle* for the UK to 'de-industrialize' (i.e. reduce the share of its total resources going into manufactures) as a consequence of North Sea oil, although there might well have been need for structural changes within manufacturing industry to meet a different composition of demand. Assuming no change in the stock of real resources available to the UK and no change in efficiency in existing use, the need of the UK to obtain its oil at a higher real cost than in 1972 implied a fall in the UK's real income as compared with that year. (Of course, the decline in the UK's real income would have been greater without North Sea oil.)

However, although by 1979–80 the UK appeared to require in a resource sense a manufacturing sector relative to its GDP probably as large as in 1972, a smaller proportion of the output of that sector had to be exported. Conversely non-oil-producing industrial countries had to devote more resources to tradables, so that the share of UK tradables/manufactures in total world trade could, *ceteris paribus*, be expected to decline. As a consequence, the UK's real exchange rate could be expected to rise somewhat in the second half of the 1970s, (even though the UK remained an importer of oil), either through a rise in the nominal exchange rate or through a rise in the UK's domestic price level as compared with price levels abroad. Although the behaviour of the UK's real exchange rate throughout the 1970s is very erratic, there does appear to have been an upward trend commencing in 1976 (see table 3.2). Moreover, despite what has been said above – that, as

**Table 3.2**   UK real effective exchange rate (1980–2 = 100)

| | |
|---|---|
| 1975 | 73.9 |
| 1976 | 70.4 |
| 1977 | 74.0 |
| 1978 | 77.6 |
| 1979 | 86.6 |
| 1980 | 99.2 |
| 1981 | 101.9 |
| 1982 | 98.5 |
| 1983 | 93.0 |
| 1984 | 89.7 |
| 1985 | 92.3 |
| 1986 | 88.3 |

*Source*: Morgan Guaranty Trust Company of New York, *World Financial Markets*.

**Table 3.3**   UK manufacturing production

|  | 1970 | 1972 | 1976 | 1979 | 1980 | 1981 | 1986 |
|---|---|---|---|---|---|---|---|
| Share in GDP | (34.0)[a] | 32.1 | 26.2 | 25.4 | 24.8 | 23.6 | 19.5 |
| Output at constant factor cost (1980 = 100) |  |  | 104.4 | 107.0 | 109.5 | 100.0 | 99.0 | 104.7 |

[a] Not strictly comparable with later years.
*Source*: *National Income and Expenditure*, Blue Book and *Economic Trends*, Central Statistical Office

compared with 1972, the UK had no need to 'de-industrialize' – the share of manufacturing in GDP showed a strong downward trend from around 32 per cent in 1972 to 25 per cent in 1979 (table 3.3). In fact, manufacturing output was very little higher in 1979 than in 1972 and well below its peak in 1973. Hence other factors were clearly operating in the UK in the 1970s, some of which have been examined in chapter 1.[5]

In the third phase (beginning 1980), the UK became self-sufficient in oil and soon afterwards a net exporter. Given self-sufficiency, the UK neither gained nor lost in an absolute resource sense from the steep rise in oil price in 1979–80, although its *relative* position compared with other industrial countries clearly further improved; but as it moved into a position of being a net exporter, it gained in an absolute sense as well and began to recuperate some of the absolute real resource loss it had suffered in the mid and late 1970s as compared with pre-1973.

The extent to which, in principle at least, it was able to draw on the resources of oil-importing countries – via the high price of oil – so as to defray part of the cost of its own oil production can be roughly estimated as follows. In 1972–3, the UK consumed and imported around 110 million tonnes of oil at an import cost of about £23 per tonne in 1980 prices: thus the total cost in that year amounted to £2,530 million in 1980 prices. By 1983 the North Sea was producing about 110 million tonnes at a cost of about £40 a tonne (1980 prices) whilst consumption amounted to about 70 million tonnes. The UK was a net exporter of about 40 million tonnes which it sold at a world price of about £120 per tonne (1980 prices). Thus the UK was in principle able to

5 Manufacturing production as a share of GDP declined in all industrial countries, with the exception of Japan, in this period.

set against the higher real resource cost of its oil [£110(40–23) million = £1,870 million] the revenue it obtained from sales of oil abroad [£40(120) million = £4,800 million]. In effect the real resource cost of oil to the UK was significantly lower (by about £3,000 million) in 1983 than in 1972.[6] Much of this gain to the UK was absorbed by a need to remit interest and dividends on past foreign investment in North Sea oil, although this in turn was offset at least temporarily by continuing high foreign investment in the sector.[7] Of course, about a third of the saving was due to oil consumption being lower in 1983 than in 1972,[8] but other countries also conserved oil though still had to devote far more resources to obtaining what they did consume as compared with 1972.

The future improvement in the UK's position relative to other industrial countries clearly strengthened the presumption that sterling's real exchange rate would tend to rise and the share of UK manufactures in the world total would tend to fall. While other industrial countries were required to increase their exports of tradables to meet higher oil bills, this was not necessary for the UK. Moreover, the fact that a part of its output of oil could be sold abroad at a price far exceeding its real domestic resource cost, implied that the UK could raise its domestic consumption of tradables relatively to its domestic production of them, thereby strengthening the presumption that the share of manufacturing in GDP would fall – and fall not only as compared with what might have had to have been the case in 1974 (if the UK had not resorted to external borrowing instead of transferring real resources to exports) but also as compared with 1972.[9]

At any rate, the UK's real exchange rate rose strongly after 1978 (table 3.2), appreciating by something like 31 per cent before peaking out in 1981.[10] The share of manufacturing in GDP fell by another four

6  Although net exports of oil continued to rise after 1983, the gain was probably offset by falling real oil price and rising cost of production. Thus 1983 was probably the best year from this point of view.

7  *UK Balance of Payments 1984*, table 9.1.

8  Abstracting from the fall in UK domestic oil consumption, the net saving to the British economy would be equal to the economic rent derived from exports, less the increased cost of domestic consumption of oil in 1973, as against what that consumption would have cost in 1972 – i.e. £40 (120–40) – £70 (40–23) million equal to £2,010 million.

9  The share of UK exports of manufacturers in OECD exports of manufactures fell from 9.8% to 7.3% over the period 1970–83. It is interesting to note however that the export share of most other major industrial countries also fell in this period, the major exception being Japan whose share rose by almost 50%. See *Economic Progress Report*, June/July 1985 (HM Treasury).

10  Not all of the rise in the real exchange rate can be attributed to oil (see chapter 4).

percentage points, whilst manufacturing output fell by over 10 per cent. The 'de-industrialization' of the UK appeared to be well on the way to becoming an accomplished fact! How far this was the expected result of Britain's newly acquired oil producer status and how far the result of the monetary and fiscal policy pursued by Mrs Thatcher's government or other factors is, of course, the main topic of the rest of this book. However, some policy implications of oil producer status can be usefully discussed here to put subsequent discussion and analysis into perspective.

## Policy Implications

North Sea oil shielded the UK from the massive rise in the world price of oil in the 1970s; indeed, by the early 1980s the country was better off with a higher price of oil *and* North Sea oil than it was in 1972 with a lower price of oil but no North Sea oil – although not by much (the earlier calculation suggests between 1 and 1½ per cent of 1980 GDP). *Given the high price of oil ruling in the early 1980s*, however, the UK was obviously much better off with North Sea oil than it would have been without it, possibly by as much as 5 per cent of 1980 GDP. Thus, even though it is somewhat misleading to say that the UK received a substantial *increment* of real income as a result of North Sea oil as compared with the position in 1972, at any rate the country's real income was significantly higher with it than without it. What use could the UK make of that advantage?

As indicated earlier in the chapter, an increment of real income presented in the form of foreign exchange can theoretically have positive multiplier effects on the economy provided that the full or greater employment of existing domestic resources is currently being constrained by a balance of payments constraint (i.e., inability to sell sufficient exports to cover more imports required at higher level of output and employment). In the case of an advanced industrial country whose major exports are in price elastic demand so that devaluation should make it possible to sell more exports, the problem must lie more in the domestic supply conditions of the economy than in some direct externally imposed constraint. In the case of these countries, a so-called balance of payments constraint can be largely reduced to a domestic supply constraint.

Leaving this aside for discussion in later chapters, we can say that the extra real income that the UK had by virtue of North Sea oil meant that consumption and/or investment (real asset formation), whether public or private, could be larger than otherwise – i.e. present and/or future living standards can be improved. Precisely how such extra income is used depends partly on the channels through which it is injected into an economy and partly on economic policy pursued by the government at the time. In the case of North Sea oil revenue, channels and policy are closely interlocked since a substantial and increasing portion of that revenue went in the first instance to the British government in the form of tax revenue: thus, in part, the impact on the economy depended on government policy with respect to expenditure, taxation and borrowing. In fact, since these oil-related revenues were handled in the same way as all other government tax revenues (i.e. pooled), it is not possible to indicate in any precise way how they were in fact used. The government's intention, as expressed through the Medium Term Financial Strategy,[11] was to reduce government expenditure, taxation and borrowing in relation to GDP, suggesting that the aim was to channel benefits to the community in the form of higher net incomes, with the expectation perhaps that greater private sector saving and lower interest rates would stimulate investment.

Of course the outcome must depend on the totality of a government's economic aims and policy as well as events external to the British economy itself. The British government has been criticized for following policies that 'wasted' oil revenue either on the grounds that those policies resulted in recession and a decline in non-oil GDP (between 1979 and 1981 real GDP including oil fell by nearly 4 per cent) or because the revenue increased consumption, both government and private, rather than investment (between 1979 and 1981–2 private plus government consumption rose by about 4 per cent despite a decline in real GDP). The aims and results of government policies in this period and later years is the subject of the following chapters, but it can be noted here that the argument that North Sea oil rent was wasted in a splurge on imports is much overdone. In fact, a major beneficiary of oil rent was the UK's balance of payments. Imports in real terms showed very little increase over the period 1979–82 (although no doubt a larger proportion of them went into domestic private consumption than earlier) and did not begin to rise significantly until 1983 when the domestic real economy was also recovering. The cumulative surplus in the UK's current account balance of payments during 1980–5 amounted to nearly £24 billion in current prices or approximately £19 billion in 1980 prices. Since the UK's realized economic rent (more strictly, the realized cash flow) from North Sea oil amounted to about £50 billion in 1980

11 See chapter 4.

prices in the same period,[12] it can be concluded that getting on for 40 per cent of the UK's net increment of real income from oil realized in those years was invested in overseas assets. The abolition of foreign exchange control in 1979 was certainly an important factor underlying the flow of capital abroad,[13] and it was an appropriate response to the coming on stream of North Sea oil, if best use was to be made of the real resources. Without it, the UK's real exchange rate would have appreciated even more.

Of course there is by no means general agreement that investment overseas was the best use of North Sea oil rent. Many take the view that investing the oil rent overseas was to the long term disadvantage of the UK since it tended to increase productive capacity overseas rather than at home. As a result the UK's competitive position in manufacturing industry has suffered, storing up severe problems for when the oil runs out. (Strangely enough, many of the people taking this view also lament the fact that the balance of trade in manufactures moved from a surplus in the UK's favour to a deficit, ignoring the obvious fact that if the UK had not invested overseas, i.e. had not run a consistent current account surplus, the deterioration in its trade position in manufactures would have been even greater!). The argument against foreign investment overlooks the relative rates of return obtainable on investment at home and investment overseas which at the private level favoured the latter. The relative *social* returns are very difficult to calculate – relying on imposed 'shadow' prices for domestic factors of production – and would imply knowledge of the future that perhaps few possess. The fact is that the actual return in terms of sterling on investment overseas has been very high. Helped by foreign asset price revaluations and particularly by sterling devaluation after 1981, the UK's net (identified) external assets (almost wholly private sector) rose by over £90 billion in 1980–6.[14]

12 See *Bank of England Quarterly Bulletin*, (December 1986), North Sea Oil and Gas, p. 514. Note that 1985 prices can be converted to 1980 prices by dividing the former by 1.4. Note also that about half of the rent earned up to the end of 1985 was passed onto consumers by setting gas prices lower than world equivalent energy prices.

13 Portfolio capital outflows rose from about £1 billion in 1978 to over £4 billion in 1981, to over £6 billion in 1983, and eventually to over £17 billion in 1985. In the three years 1979–81 when sterling was rising strongly, portfolio capital outflows aggregated over £8 billion whilst inflows amounted to just over £3 billion. See *UK Balance of Payments 1987* (Central Statistical Office).

14 See *Bank of England Quarterly Bulletin*, (Nov. 1987), External Balance Sheet of the UK, table H.

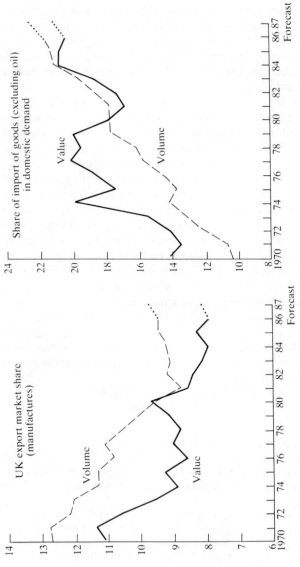

**Figure 3.1** Export shares and import penetration

*Source: Financial Statement and Budget Report, 1987–8, chart 3.6*

It is evident that North Sea oil posed problems as well as opportunities for the UK economy, and it would be a mistake to disregard the nature of them in any assessment of the conduct and results of policy. Whether or not (or rather, at what standard of living) the UK can survive the eventual and inevitable exhaustion of oil reserves[15] depends on how the advantage of having them was employed; but it depends much more on how the potential economic performance of the UK has been affected by economic policy in its totality, which is the subject of the remainder of this book.

Here it can be simply noted that the massive fall in oil price that took place through 1985 (from $28 a barrel to $15, at one point to barely $10), which halved the UK's surplus on oil trade (from £8 billion to £4 billion) seems to have been absorbed without the serious ill effects that many had feared. Indeed since the peaking out of real oil price in 1982 and the subsequent and expected fall in the UK's real exchange rate, the UK's share in volume terms of developed countries' exports' of manufactures has been rising, in strong contrast to the precipitate decline through the 1970s. The share in terms of *value*, although continuing to fall in the early 1980s, by 1987 showed signs of stabilizing (see figure 3.1). Export performance was particularly impressive in the twelve months prior to the general election of 1987, and in the first quarter of that year the current account of the balance of payments remained in substantial surplus despite a large fall in revenue from oil. Although 1987 as a whole seemed likely to see the current account in deficit, following near balance in 1986 and substantial surpluses in the previous six years, there is at the time of writing no good reason for believing that the UK faces serious crisis.[16]

15 Although inevitable, the exhaustion of Britain's oil reserves is by no means imminent. A recent estimate suggests that at least as much oil remains in North Sea fields as has been extracted so far. See *Financial Times*, 7 Sept. 1987.

16 In fact, owing to substantial under-recording of 'invisibles', the UK probably has a much better balance of payments position than officially recorded.

# 4

# Implementation and Results of the Strategy

This chapter provides a brief account of the implementation and results of the Thatcher strategy during the period 1979–87, leaving it to later chapters for criticism and overall assessment.

The Medium Term Financial Strategy (MTFS) – the centre-piece of the Thatcher government's new economic strategy – was introduced in the budget of 1980, after the government had been in power for almost a year. But the earlier budget of June 1979 was significant in its own right, since steps were taken in it that probably had a greater impact on the economy than the MTFS itself.

## Fiscal and Monetary Policy 1979–80

The government had inherited from the previous Labour administration a projected budget deficit of over £9 billion, i.e. over 5 per cent of GDP, for the fiscal year 1978/9. Although committed to achieving a better budget balance, the new government's first move in this direction was relatively minor, the aim being to cut the deficit by about £1 billion in 1979–80, bringing it closer to 4.5 per cent of GDP. Much more important were proposed changes to the structure of the tax system, involving a major shift from direct to indirect taxation. The standard rate of tax was reduced from 33 per cent to 30 per cent whilst the marginal tax rate on earned income was reduced from 83 per cent to 60 per cent. (Eight years later the standard rate had been reduced to 27 per cent and the top marginal tax rate to 40 per cent.) Value Added Tax (VAT) was raised from a range of 10–12 per cent to a uniform 15 per cent, offsetting the loss of revenue from direct taxes. Whilst such a change in the structure of taxation could be (and was) attacked on income distribution grounds, it was in line with the Conservative party's declared aim of increasing incentives. Admittedly, the regressiveness of the shift from direct to indirect taxation was lessened by the omission of certain essential items of expenditure, such as food, from VAT; but even so, the initial once-for-all impact on the consumer price level was of the order of 3 per cent. The shift therefore attracted criticism on grounds that it exacerbated inflation which it was the government's declared intention to fight. The overall stance of the budget also attracted the opposition of those economists, bedded deep in the Keynesian tradition, who believed that the macroeconomic situation (unemployment exceeding 1 million) required a larger budget deficit rather than a smaller one; but this of course cut no ice with a government which had made it clear that it had forsworn short run Keynesian demand management.

Whilst the 'inflation promoting' charge against the VAT increase could be rejected in principle – on grounds that it simply brought about a once-for-all rise in the price level rather than set the scene for continued faster inflation – it is difficult to believe that subsequent wage pressure was unaffected. Moreover, rightly or wrongly, in the course of the run-up to the election, the incoming government had openly committed itself to implementing the public sector pay recommendations of the Commission on Pay Comparability chaired by Professor Clegg. Increases in pay varying between 16 and 25 per cent was awarded to public sector officials, imposing directly or indirectly further once-for-all upward pressure on the price level. Thus a combination of inherited inflationary pressure originating in 1977–8, VAT increase and Clegg public sector pay awards ensured a substantial rise in the price level in the course of 1979. By the end of that year, inflation was running at an annual rate of over 20 per cent, compared with around 10 per cent a year earlier. But the significance of this big jump in inflation lay less in the fact that anti-inflation policy already seemed to have broken down, than in the problem it imposed for monetary policy, and the consequent pressure it placed on the real economy.

As far as monetary policy was concerned, the new government found no philosophical difficulty in continuing the practice of setting monetary aggregate targets first introduced by the previous Labour administration; and a target range of 7–11 per cent for Sterling M3 (£M3)[1] was

1 Defined as notes and coin and non-interest and interest bearing sight deposits with banks, plus UK private sector sterling time deposits with banks.

set for 1979–80. But the inconsistency between the 'once-for-all' price increase that was in the pipeline for 1979–80 and the projected increase in the money supply was, if not *ex ante*, certainly *ex post*, apparent, and indeed became evident through 1979–80 itself. The attempt to keep Sterling M3 within its target range necessitated repeated increases in interest rates, Minimum lending rate (MLR) being raised from its starting level of 12 per cent in April 1979 to 17 per cent in November. Even so, the increase in Sterling M3 in the course of fiscal 1979/80 exceeded the upper limit of its target range by over 1 per cent.[2]

The most dramatic development through 1979–80 was a strong appreciation of sterling. In *nominal* terms, the trade weighted rate (the so-called effective rate) had begun to rise in the last few months of 1978, largely because of a weak dollar; and, with but a short interruption in early 1979, this continued strongly through 1979 and most of 1980. By the end of 1980, the UK's *nominal* effective exchange rate had appreciated by over 25 per cent as compared with the end of 1978, and the *real* exchange rate (i.e., the nominal rate adjusted for inflation in the UK and its major trading partners) by over 30 per cent. It seemed surprising to many commentators at the time, that Sterling rose so strongly in 1979 and 1980 when money supply as measured by Sterling M3 was increasing fast, well outside its target range. It can be argued that, in the circumstances of the time, the stance of monetary policy could not be adequately measured by the behaviour of Sterling M3. The combination of rising interest rates and exchange rates, which imposed a massive squeeze on UK manufacturing industry, tended to increase distress borrowing by firms, and therefore to increase bank lending and money supply (Sterling M3) rather than reduce it. In such circumstances the relative tightness of monetary policy could perhaps be better judged by the behaviour of a narrower definition of money supply such as M1 or M0[3] which was much more closely related to transactions demand for money and therefore to the behaviour of nominal income (see later in this chapter and in chapter 5).

It is certainly true that the rate of increase in M0 (see figure 4.1) slowed down sharply through 1979 and 1980, from over 15 per cent at the end of 1978 to barely 5 per cent at the end of 1980. In fact, real

2 During this period Sterling M3 was constrained by the so-called 'corset', i.e. regulations governing commercial bank supply of interest bearing deposits (IBEL) imposed in 1973.

3 M0 includes notes and coin and operational bankers' balances at the Bank of England. M1 includes non-interest bearing deposits with banks in addition.

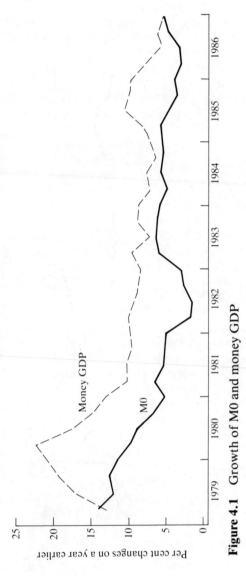

**Figure 4.1** Growth of M0 and money GDP

*Source: Financial Statement and Budget Report, 1987–8, (HM Treasury, March 1987)*

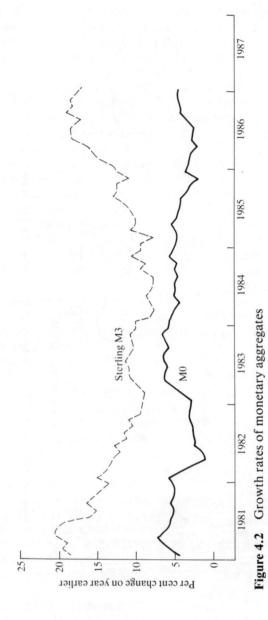

**Figure 4.2**  Growth rates of monetary aggregates

*Source: Financial Statement and Budget Report, 1987–8, (HM Treasury, March 1987)*

M0 (i.e. nominal M0 deflated by the price level) actually declined through much of this period. During the same period, the rate of increase of Sterling M3 approached 20 per cent (see figure 4.2), even though, as mentioned earlier (footnote 2), the rise in interest bearing deposits was constrained by the 'corset' control until it was abolished in mid 1980. The 'corset' constraint on interest bearing eligible liabilities (IBELs) constrained the commercial banks' ability to lend, leading to some disintermediation of the banks as thwarted borrowers went to other financial institutions, including foreign banks.

Although the decline in the rate of increase of nominal and real M0 may have been a truer measure of monetary tightness than Sterling M3, it cannot be argued that it was the proximate causal force behind the output recession which soon hit the UK (see figure 4.3): in fact, the rate of increase of *nominal* GDP accelerated through 1979 – thus breaking the normally expected close relationship between money GDP and M0 (figure 4.1) – and did not decline until 1980, when it did so sharply. Clearly the decisive causal factor underlying the serious recession that began in 1980 was the rise in sterling's real exchange rate.[4] Undoubtedly, this was related to high interest rates and domestic monetary squeeze. However, as indicated in chapter 3, the fact that in the late 1970s the UK was rapidly becoming self-sufficient in oil, and soon after a net exporter, at a time when the world price of oil also rose substantially, could be expected to lead to a significant rise in the UK's real exchange rate, independently of any effect exerted through monetary policy. (Easier monetary policy aimed at keeping down the *nominal* exchange rate would simply have resulted in more inflation without effect on the real exchange rate.) Moreover, possible confidence effects (the so-called Thatcher effect) engendered by the coming into power of a Conservative government committed to restructuring monetary and fiscal policies may also have encouraged capital inflows. On the other hand, the government liberalized foreign exchange control in the course of 1979 and finally abolished it in October of that year; and this *cet. par.* would have operated to temper the rise in the real exchange rate since outflows of capital were then permitted. Portfolio capital outflows were certainly encouraged, rising from about £1 billion in 1978 to over £4 billion in 1981 (over £6 billion in 1983). In the three critical years 1979–81 when sterling was rising strongly, portfolio capital outflows aggregated over £8 billion whilst inflows aggregated about

---

4 However, it should be noted that other major industrial countries soon followed the UK into recession so that not all of Britain's problems at this time can be attributed solely to the behaviour of the exchange rate.

£3 billion. However, although capital outflows would have tended to mitigate the rise in the real exchange rate, abolition of exchange control may have contributed to domestic monetary squeeze.

It is difficult if not impossible to allocate relative importance to monetary squeeze on the one hand and oil factor and confidence effects on the other. Some economists put most weight on the former, others on the latter. An informed Treasury guess is that oil-related factors may have contributed between a half and two-thirds of the 30 per cent rise in the UK's real exchange rate between 1978 and 1981.[5] However, it is clear that the fiscal and monetary policy mix was significant, and the question arises whether that policy was correct or not. We shall return to this question in the next chapter, which examines criticisms of macroeconomic policy in the Thatcher period.

## Introduction of MTFS in 1980

Although not yet obvious in inflation and output terms, policy was clearly having a significant impact on the economy before the MTFS was formally launched in the budget of 1980. Table 4.1 sets out the proposed targets for the public sector borrowing requirement (PSBR) and money supply over a four-year period.

Buttressing these targets and presumably giving credibility to them were projected public spending plans and implied tax revenues. The stated objective of the strategy was the gradual reduction of inflation and a progressive but not precipitate return to budget balance. Clearly the government had no intention of going for 'shock' treatment, although *ex post* it can be fairly argued that the 'shock' had already taken place before the MFTS saw the light of the day.

Although forecasts made at the time of the 1980 budget suggested that the UK (and indeed the rest of the world) was moving into

**Table 4.1**   MTFS targets in the 1980 budget

|  | *1980/1* | *1981/2* | *1982/3* | *1983/4* |
|---|---|---|---|---|
| PSBR as a % of GDP | 3.75 | 3.0 | 2.25 | 1.5 |
| Sterling M3 (% increase) | 7–11 | 6–10 | 5–9 | 4–8 |

5  For a recent examination of the impact of North Sea oil on the exchange rate see Charles Bean, *Sterling Misalignment and British Trade Performance* (CEPR Discussion Paper no. 177, May 1987).

recession, the 1980 budget planned for a cut in the 1980-1 PSBR by about £0.5 billion, bringing it down from a realized 4.75 per cent of GDP in the earlier year to 3.75 per cent of GDP as set out in the strategy. Moreover, despite obvious difficulties in containing the growth of Sterling M3, the strategy involved keeping the same target range of 7-11 per cent increase for 1980/1 as was proposed for 1979/80. It was soon clear, however, that the economic situation in the UK would not permit achievement of either PSBR or money supply target. Owing to deterioration in nationalized industry finances and increasing welfare and other benefits, planned public expenditure was soon exceeded. As for the money supply target, this was quickly abandoned (although not formally) as the government came to recognize the apparent misleading behaviour of Sterling M3. No attempt was made to achieve the target by raising interest rates as had been done in the autumn of 1979; instead, interest rates were lowered. Minimum Lending Rate was cut by 1 per cent in July 1980 and a further 2 per cent in November and the 'corset' control over IBELs was abolished. An inquiry was set in train by the Treasury and the Bank of England, focusing on the behaviour, relevance and means of controlling the monetary aggregates, and a Green Paper on monetary control was issued towards the end of the year. This naturally concluded that the behaviour of Sterling M3 could be, and in fact had been in 1979/80, misleading, and recommended that the behaviour of other aggregates should be taken into account when assessing monetary conditions. For obvious reasons, the Treasury did not formally forsake its Sterling M3 target even though, with the abolition of the 'corset', Sterling M3 was rising fast. Still, it was evidently clear that the Treasury intended to take a wider view of the behaviour of monetary aggregates,[6] and there was perhaps some indication that sterling's exchange rate would also enter into the assessment.

In an institutional sense, changes were made in the method of monetary control. The object was to give the Bank of England somewhat less control over longer term interest rates, and market influence more. Discount window lending by the Bank of England was to be reduced in favour of open market operations in the Treasury and Commercial bill market aimed at keeping short term (7-day) interest rates within an unpublished 2 per cent band. However, it is doubtful whether these significantly affected the thrust of monetary policy.

Although in terms of the wider aggregate Sterling M3 and in terms of nominal interest rates, monetary policy seemed less restrictive in 1980

6 The Treasury turned first to M1 and later to M0.

than in the second half of 1979, the UK's nominal and real exchange rate continued to appreciate strongly, and it did not peak out until the end of the year. By now the UK was in steep recession, real GDP having fallen by about 3.5 per cent between the fourth quarters of 1979 and 1980. Manufacturing production was down even more sharply. Hence much indignation was raised by the budget of 1981 which, far from loosening fiscal policy, significantly tightened it.

## The 1981 Budget

As indicated earlier, the government had found it impossible to implement the MTFS's first year target for the PSBR. Instead of a planned deficit of £8.5 billion (3.75 per cent of GDP) for the fiscal year 1980-1, the actual outcome was nearer £13 billion or 5.7 per cent of GDP. Since the MTFS's money supply target had also been exceeded by at least 10 per cent, the strategy appeared to be in tatters. The aim of demonstrating that it was still alive and kicking no doubt underlay the budget that was produced!

The government set a target of £10.5 billion for the PSBR (4.25 per cent of projected GDP), some £3 billion less than the outcome for 1980-1, and £4 billion less than on existing tax rates and and expenditure plans was forecast for 1981/2. Increases in taxes were to bear the main brunt of the adjustment, the main proposals being the non-indexation of tax thresholds and most allowances (involving a substantial real reduction) thereby raising direct taxes, an increase in indirect taxes (largely excise taxes but not VAT) and a once-for-all tax on commercial banks' current accounts. In addition to tightening the stance of fiscal policy, and despite the difficulties with Sterling M3, the government set lower targets for this aggregate, at 6-10 per cent, than had been either aimed for or achieved in the previous two years. However the government was able to lower minimum lending rate by 2 per cent, indicating some proposed easing of monetary restriction.

A severe tightening of fiscal policy – although clearly aimed at creating the conditions that would permit some loosening of monetary policy – at a time when the UK was in its most serious post-war economic recession could not go by unrebuked. The UK economics profession reacted most strongly and 364 economists, including a number of past chief economic advisers to previous governments – but not all past deputy chief economic advisers[7] – signed a letter to *The*

7 See letter to the *Financial Times*, 3 Apr. 1981 signed by Professor Maynard and Professor Rose for a contrary view to that expressed by the 364.

*Times* (31 March 1981) in protest. The letter affirmed among other things that 'Present policies will deepen the depression, erode the industrial base of our economy and threaten its social and political stability'. In retrospect the timing of the letter proved to be inapt – it would perhaps have looked better if it had appeared in 1979 – since the first quarter of 1981 proved to be close to the low point of the economy (figure 4.3). Output, including manufacturing, rose in the remainder of the year and continued to do so through the next seven years. It has to be said that recovery followed a sharp fall (10 per cent in 6 months) in sterling's effective exchange rate, in both nominal and real terms. Whether this weakening of sterling was a response to monetary ease or due to a more realistic appraisal of oil price and the UK's North Sea oil prospects cannot easily be said.[8] Against the monetary argument was the fact that the rate of increases of both broad money (Sterling M3) and narrow money (M0) *declined* through 1981 (figures 4.1 and 4.2); on the other hand, sterling M3 was still increasing at a faster rate than had been targeted for at the time of the budget. Undoubtedly, in the fall in sterling and in the apparently still fast growth of money supply there were grounds for unease in capital markets which could prejudice the government's funding programme. At any rate the government responded by raising interest rates so that by the second half of the year, minimum lending rate was back to 16 per cent. The fall in sterling was temporarily stayed and monetary growth was brought closer to target. Interest rates were quickly brought down again and by the time of the 1982 budget, minimum lending rate was back to 13 per cent. Despite a further weakening in sterling in the course of 1982, interest rates continued to fall, with minimum lending rate being fixed at 9 per cent in November of the year (see figure 4.6).

The 1981 budget was conspicuous not only because it introduced a severe fiscal squeeze at a time of recession but also because it reverted to the much earlier practice of controlling public expenditure through cash limits. With the acceleration of inflation through the late 1960s and the decade of the 1970s, governments of all complexions had turned to the practice of planning government expenditure at fixed prices (in Treasury jargon of the time, 'survey' prices), i.e. in real terms. In effect government departments asked for and were guaranteed quantities of real resources – equipment, personnel, etc. – irrespective of the money price that would have to be paid at the time of use. Actual money

8 The fall in sterling cannot be explained simply by the strengthening of the dollar following the tightening of monetary policy in the US, since sterling also fell against the Deutschmark.

expenditure therefore was open-ended and depended on the price at the time. Thus government spending departments were protected from inflation – not only general inflation but also particular inflation applying to the particular resources they were using, which usually tends to be greater than general inflation. Of course, there was some logic behind the method but it did mean that the Treasury had no idea what government expenditure would be in money terms, and would have to be financed out of taxation or borrowing, until after the event. Nor was there any pressure on spending departments to make more efficient use of resources if the price level of these resources rose, or indeed, to make some effort to keep prices down. The return to cash limits meant not that that real resource planning was abolished but that, once the real resource allocation had been agreed for a coming period and the cash expenditure calculated at current prices, only a general expected inflation factor could be applied to the totals to fix the cash limits for the spending period. But given this restriction, the Treasury has a firm idea of what money expenditure will be; moreover, spending departments can be put under strong pressure to contain their own costs. However it should be noted that cash control limits apply only to public expenditure on goods and services and not to transfer expenditure (i.e. Social Security benefits, etc.).

Although attacked as irrational by many economists, the new practice could and can still be defended on at least two grounds: first, that it tended to act as an automatic inflation stabilizer (since if general inflation exceeded that built into the expenditure forecasts and limits, real public expenditure and therefore *cet. par.* aggregate demand would be *pari passu* reduced); and second, that it gave ministers and public sector officials and trade unions an incentive to support disinflationary policies.

Although heavily criticized at the time, the 1981 budget was probably crucial for the MTFS: it seemed to establish beyond doubt the government's determination to pursue its anti-inflation policy.[9] The realized PSBR for 1981/2 (as a percentage of GDP) turned out to be less than projected at the time of the budget and not much higher than had been targeted at the inception of the strategy. Also, the increase in £M3 through 1981/2 was only slightly above the upper end of the range established at the time of the budget. Moreover, despite apparent fiscal and monetary squeeze, real GDP showed some rise in the course of the year, as did industrial and manufacturing production. The rate of

9 In current jargon, it established 'credibility', now recognized by economic theorists to be a key factor for effectiveness.

inflation came down markedly, the retail price level having risen by barely 4 per cent between the first quarters of 1981 and 1982.

Of course, it can be argued that the substantial fall in the UK's real exchange rate was the main factor behind this recovery, and that in any case easier fiscal and monetary policy would have resulted in an even larger rise in output. Even so, the dire warnings of the 364 economists proved unwarranted and some at least must have felt discomfited.

## Budgets after 1981

The progress of the fiscal element of the MTFS after the 1981 budget was less eventful although the strategy was always under attack for being too restrictive. Indeed budgets after 1981 were probably more conspicuous for their intended micro-effects than for their macro-economic stance.

The 1982 budget aimed at (and succeeded in getting *ex post*) a small reduction in PSBR as a percentage of GDP. Its conspicuous features were a 1 per cent reduction in the National Insurance Surcharge (from 3.5 per cent to 2.5 per cent), which could be welcomed because a tax on labour use seemed particularly inappropriate at a time of excess supply of labour; and raising tax thresholds by 2 per cent more than the rate of inflation was welcome also because it could increase the willingness of unemployed people to seek work at a given money wage. The 1982 budget also introduced the principle of at least partial indexation for inflation of capital gains, and this too was welcome because it could provide encouragement to the providers of equity capital, particularly for small business.

The pre-election budget of 1983 went further in reducing real tax thresholds by raising the tax exemption limit by 14 per cent when a 5.5 per cent increase would have been sufficient to offset the previous year's inflation. There was a small increase in the National Insurance contribution but this was accompanied by a further 0.5 per cent reduction in the National Insurance Surcharge. Other measures, for example the introduction of the Business Expansion Scheme aimed at the encouragement of small business, were also included. At the macro level, a small reduction in the PSBR from the 1982/3 outcome of 3.75 per cent of GDP to 2.75 per cent for 1983/4 was projected, but not only was this not achieved *ex post*, a mid-year reduction in some cash-controlled expenditure and substantial asset sales (see later) were required to prevent the realized PSBR ratio from rising above the previous year's level.

The 1984 budget set out to cut the PSBR substantially, from the outcome of £9.7 billion in 1983/4, to £7 billion or an expected 2.25 per cent of GDP for 1984/5. In fact, the Treasury had in mind containing the PSBR at that level for the next four years, and reducing the ratio to GDP from 3.25 per cent in 1983/4 to 1.75 per cent in 1988/9. The miners' strike intervened, adding significantly to public expenditure in both 1984 and 1985. The government did not attempt to offset this by raising taxes or cutting other expenditure, so that the PSBR out-turn for 1984/5 exceeded £10 billion (just over 3 per cent of GDP as in the previous fiscal year).

However, the 1984 budget was significant for its welcome proposals to reform the corporate tax system. As indicated in chapter 1, the system had, through a system of generous tax allowances, subsidized investment in plant and machinery and industrial buildings on a generous scale from the mid 1960s on. Although aimed at producing a higher rate of investment and therefore faster growth, the practice could be criticized on a number of grounds, in particular that it encouraged wasteful investment with a low rate of return and that, taken in conjunction with the high taxes imposed on labour through the National Insurance contribution and National Insurance Surcharge, contributed to an excessive substitution of capital for labour, and therefore to rising unemployment. (For reasons examined in chapter 1, it also contributed to the country's balance of payments problems.) There is little indication that previous attempts to improve the UK industrial performance by subsidies to investment were at all successful. In fact the international evidence seems to suggest that tax subsidies to investment in manufacturing industry is inversely related to economic performance.[10]

Thus the government had strong grounds for reforming the system; and the 1984 budget proposed that first year tax allowances for investment in plant and machinery and in industrial and agricultural buildings should be progressively reduced – in the case of plant and machinery, from the existing 100 per cent to 25 per cent in 1986. Only investment in Enterprise Zones escaped,[11] since the government wished to encourage

---

10 The following figures of tax subsidy rates on manufacturing fixed investment, from *Lloyds Bank Review*, are interesting. The US and the UK which subsidized investment most had poorer growth performance than Japan and Germany which did not subsidize fixed investment in manufacturing. The figures represent the rates as a percentage of asset price: UK 13.1, US 12.8, Netherlands 6.2, Italy 5.0, France 4.4, Japan – 3.4, Germany – 5.5.

11 See *Enterprise Zone Policy Proposal* (Dept of the Environment, 1980).

small business and employment in particular areas of the country. At the same time, the corporate tax rate was reduced from 50 per cent in 1983 to 35 per cent in 1986. These measures were conducive to efficient rather than wasteful investment and to raising the productivity of the existing capital stock over time. Other measures were proposed to promote industrial innovation, and the excess tax on labour use – the National Insurance Surcharge – was further reduced.

The 1985 budget was conspicuous for its emphasis on job promotion. At the fiscal level, employers' and employees' National Insurance contributions for lowest paid workers were cut from 9 per cent to a range of 5–7 per cent, whilst the upper earnings limit on employers' contribution was abolished (so that, in effect, beyond a certain income level, the implicit payroll tax became a proportional tax at the top end). (It was expected that as a result of the change in the structure of the National Insurance contribution firms would save £900 million on the 8.5 million people employed at less than £130 a week.) Basic income tax thresholds were raised by 10 per cent (i.e. by double the rate of inflation), substantially reducing average tax rates on low pay.

Other measures, including some of a non-fiscal kind, were proposed to improve prospects for job creation. It was proposed to expand Youth Training Schemes and community programmes,[12] and to review the operation of Wages Councils which, it was thought, tended to keep minimum wages too high, thereby discouraging employment. Also, it was proposed to change existing legislation governing unfair dismissal claims which it was thought discouraged employers from taking on new labour. Other measures included 100 per cent first year allowances for scientific research and inflation indexing of capital gains.

At the macro level, the 1985 budget set a PSBR target of £7 billion, as compared with the £10.2 billion outcome for 1984/5, implying a very sharp fall in the ratio to GDP. Thus the government appeared to be determined to put its MTFS back on course. Even so, there were signs that the government's attitude towards macroeconomic policy was shifting, in the sense that it seemed to be becoming more agnostic on the question whether monetary or fiscal policy was the key. Also, in his budget statement the Chancellor indicated that the exchange rate would assume greater significance in policy making.

This shift in emphasis was increasingly evident in the 1986 budget. For the first time, an expectation (not a target!) of nominal GDP growth was included in the Financial Statement and Budget Report which also stated that 'Economic Policy is set in a nominal framework

12  See later for reference to these schemes.

in which public expenditure is controlled in cash terms and money GDP growth is gradually reduced by fiscal and monetary policy.'[13] The PSBR outcome for 1985/6 (£5.9 billion) was well short of the target announced in the 1985 budget (£7 billion) which was reaffirmed for the following four fiscal years. A decline in the ratio to GDP from 2 per cent in 1985/6 to 1.5 per cent in 1989/90 was envisaged. Thus the government aimed at maintaining the credibility of its anti-inflationary stance. However, adjusted for sales of assets (see later), the 1986 budget probably provided a small *ex ante* fiscal boost to the economy.

Despite an anticipated substantial fall in revenue from North Sea oil, due to the steep fall in oil price which had taken place since the beginning of the year,[14] the budget still aimed at a small reduction in the real burden of tax. Unlike the previous budget, priority was given to reducing the basic rate of tax, which was cut from 30p to 29p. Most personal tax allowances were raised in line with inflation but no more. Although the 1986 budget continued to emphasize 'job creation', no further cuts were made in the National Insurance contribution (the tax on labour); instead, the government preferred to spend relatively small amounts of money on job promotion schemes. In particular, a new subsidy for low paid jobs for 18–20 year olds[15] and a variety of job counselling and job start schemes were expanded or started. Other measures were also announced: for example, the introduction of a Personal Equity Plan which gave tax encouragement to the purchase of shares in industry, and further expansion of the Enterprise Allowance Scheme which assists people to set up small businesses. Thus, as with the 1985 budget, micro-measures aimed at job creation rather than macroeconomic stance characterized the 1986 budget.

In the run up to the 1987 (March) budget, the outlook for public sector finance appeared unexpectedly favourable. Despite a substantial fall in tax revenue from North Sea oil amounting to £7 billion as compared with 1985–6 – due to the 1985 steep fall in the price of oil – the PSBR amounted to only £4 billion as compared with a target of £7 billion set in the 1986 budget. Increased revenue from VAT and from corporation tax,[16] the product of a buoyant economy and booming

13 *Financial Statement and Budget Report, 1986–7* (HM Treasury, Mar. 1987), para. 2.02.

14 The Brent spot price of oil fell from $28 a barrel to below $15.

15 Under the scheme, a £15 a week subsidy would be paid to employers of 18–19 year olds at up to £55 a week, and to employers of 20 year olds, at up to £65 a week.

16 The revenue gains from the change in the structure of corporate tax

profits, accounted for the difference. Even allowing for a substantial boost to public expenditure in 1987/8 – announced in the previous November – the government appeared to have substantial room, amounting to around £5.5 billion, for cuts in taxes or public sector borrowing. Despite the electoral opportunities provided by an almost certain immediate pre-election budget, the government stuck to the fiscal element of its MTFS: taxes were cut by £2.6 billion – made available by a 2 per cent cut in basic rate – and the PSBR target for 1987/8 was set at £4 billion, a £3 billion reduction from the target set in the 1986 budget. The government thus reached the objective of a PSBR equal to 1 per cent of GDP initially proposed in the MTFS. However, no other measures of a microeconomic nature were introduced in this budget.

Thus, by the end of its eighth year in office, the government could legitimately claim that it had fully implemented the fiscal side of its MTFS: the PSBR had been reduced from over 5 per cent of GDP to 1 per cent (see table 4.3). However, the anticipated effects on interest rates had not appeared – which of course raises questions concerning the rationale of the strategy at the outset.

In this connection it should be noted that fiscal policy after 1982 was more expansionary than the PSBR targets suggested. Proceeds from the sales of public sector assets (see later) were budgeted as negative expenditure rather than, as some thought they should be, financing flows.[17] Table 4.2 compares the recorded PSBRs and public sector financial deficits (PSFDs)[18] for the period 1979/80 to 1986/87 from which it can be seen that asset sales made a substantial contribution, amounting to about one-half of the recorded PSBRs for 1983/4 to 1986/7, towards the financing of public expenditure. Thus the PSFD as a proportion of GDP fell much less than did the PSBR – from 4 per cent of GDP in 1979/80 to 3 per cent in 1986/7 (Table 4.3). Of course, sales of public sector assets (privatization), aimed at increasing efficiency and performance, were an integral and announced part of the

---

introduced in the 1984 budget – i.e. abolition of tax allowances on capital spending and reduction in basic corporate tax from 50% to 35% – became apparent. The economic benefit was also becoming apparent in better quality, more productive investment.

17  It is obviously more sensible from the economic point of view to include revenue from asset sales as a form of financing since sales of assets compete in financial markets with sales of public sector debt.

18  I.e., the PSBR plus sales of public sector assets minus purchases of assets.

**Table 4.2** Public sector borrowing (PSBR) and financial deficit (PSFD) (£ billion)

|        | PSBR  | PSFD |
|--------|-------|------|
| 1979/80 | 10.0  | 8.2  |
| 1980/1  | 12.7  | 11.9 |
| 1981/2  | 8.6   | 5.8  |
| 1982/3  | 8.9   | 8.5  |
| 1983/4  | 9.7   | 12.4 |
| 1984/5  | 10.2  | 14.5 |
| 1985/6  | 5.8   | 8.2  |
| 1986/7  | 3.4   | 9.4  |
| 1987/8  | −3.5  | 2.1  |

**Table 4.3** Public sector expenditure and borrowing as percentage of GDP

|        | Public Sector Expenditure | PSBR[a] | PSFD[b] |
|--------|---------------------------|---------|---------|
| 1979/80 | 43.5   | 4.8  | 4.2 |
| 1980/1  | 46.0   | 5.4  | 5.4 |
| 1981/2  | 46.5   | 5.3  | 2.9 |
| 1982/3  | 46.75  | 3.1  | 3.8 |
| 1983/4  | 45.75  | 3.2  | 4.6 |
| 1984/5  | 46.25  | 3.1  | 4.8 |
| 1985/6  | 44.5   | 1.6  | 2.9 |
| 1986/7  | 43.75  | 0.9  | 3.1 |
| 1987/8  | 41.5   | −0.7 | 0.5 |

[a] Public Sector Borrowing Requirement
[b] Public Sector Finance Deficit (i.e. PSBR adjusted for public sector asset sales).

overall strategy of the government when it came into power; but by making demands on capital markets, it probably meant that monetary policy was in effect tighter than it would otherwise have been.

It is also important to note that comparative success with its PSBR strategy was not accompanied by similar success with plans for government expenditure. The government started out with the intention of containing public expenditure in real terms and reducing it as a proportion of GDP. But central government expenditure increased by some 15 per cent (a little more if privatization proceeds are excluded) from 1978/9 to 1987/8, and it was not until 1987/8 that expenditure as a proportion of GDP edged below the starting point of 1979/80 (table 4.3). Nonetheless the ratio of expenditure to GDP had fallen from its peak in 1982/3 when the Falklands War was imposing its demands, so that the government could clearly claim some success in this direction.

## Monetary Policy after 1981

The government had more problems with the monetary side of its strategy than with the fiscal side.

As can be seen from figure 4.2, the rate of increase of Sterling M3, which had shot up in 1980 following the abolition of the 'corset', began to decline through 1981–2, and by the end of 1982 was roughly in line with the target set in the 1982 budget (although of course, well out of line with the target set in 1980 when the MTFS was launched). (See table 4.4.). Sterling M3 appeared to give rise to no cause for concern through 1983–4, although at the upper end of the target band; but through 1985 and 1986, targets were greatly exceeded. By mid 1986, Sterling M3 was growing just as fast (at around 20 per cent per annum) as it had done in the second half of 1980. On the other hand, the rate of increase of M0, which had picked up following the low point reached in mid 1982, continued to be moderate and stayed within a target band first established in the 1984 budget. The fact that the rate of increase of nominal GDP remained well below 10 per cent, and indeed declined sharply in 1986, while inflation also continued to decline (figure 4.3), forced the government to give much less weight to Sterling M3 behaviour when formulating its macroeconomic policy stance than had been envisaged when the MTFS was launched. Certainly the government had no wish to repeat the experience of 1979–80 by bringing Sterling M3 into target range by a rise in interest rates. Even though these had fallen sharply since the third quarter of 1981, long term rates were still well above 10 per cent in 1983 and short term rates not much below (see figure 4.6).

Problems of interpreting and controlling the behaviour of Sterling M3 will be referred to in chapter 5. It is sufficient to note here that although target ranges for this aggregate were included in the budgets of 1984, 1985 and 1986, this was for 'illustrative' purposes only.[19] Even this practice was abandoned in the budget presentation in 1987, although the government still affirmed its intention to take the behaviour of broad money into account in assessing monetary conditions.[20]

19 *Financial Statement and Budget Report, 1986–7*, paras. 2.13, 2.14, 2.15.

**Table 4.4**  Money supply targets and outcomes (% increase)

| | 1981/2 | 1982/3 | 1983/4 | 1984/5 | 1985/6 | 1986/7 | 1987/8 | 1988/9 |
|---|---|---|---|---|---|---|---|---|
| **1982 budget target** | | | | | | | | |
| £M3 | | 8–12 | | | | | | |
| Outcome £M3 | | 11 | | | | | | |
| **1983 budget target** | | | | | | | | |
| £M3 | | | 7–11 | 6–10 | 5–9 | | | |
| Outcome £M3 | | | 10.1 | 13.4 | 15.3 | | | |
| **1984 budget target** | | | | | | | | |
| MO | | | | 4–8 | 3–7 | 2–6 | 1–5 | 0–4 |
| £M3 | | | | 6–10 | 5–9 | 4–8 | 3–7 | 2–6 |
| Outcome MO | | | 5.6 | 3.1 | 4.3 | | | |
| Outcome £M3 | | | | 13.4 | 15.3 | | | |
| **1985 budget target** | | | | | | | | |
| MO | | | | | | | | |
| £M3 | | | | | | | | |
| Outcome MO | | | | | | | | |
| Outcome £M3 | | | | | | | | |
| **1986 budget target** | | | | | | | | |
| MO | | | | | | 2–6 | | |
| £M3 | | | | | | 11–15 | | |
| Outcome MO | | | | | | 4 | | |
| Outcome £M3 | | | | | | | | |
| **1987 budget target** | | | | | | | | |
| MO | | | | | | | 2–6 | 1–5 |
| £M3 | | | | | | | a | |

a No target established.

*Source:* Financial Statements and Budget Reports

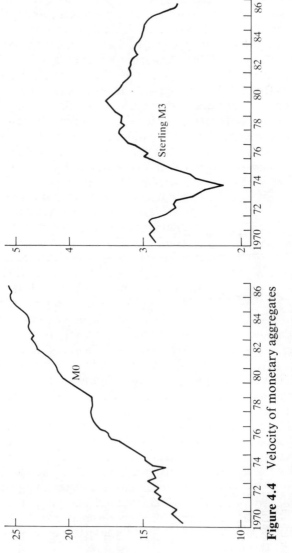

**Figure 4.4**   Velocity of monetary aggregates

*Source: Financial Statement and Budget Report, 1987–8*

M0 assumed the 'pride of place', and as indicated earlier, a target for it was established first in the 1984 budget and then in subsequent budgets (table 4.4). Of course, the Treasury was searching for a monetary aggregate which would reflect those assets (principally non-interest bearing) that are directly used for transactions, which would respond unambiguously but not oversensitively to interest rate changes, and which would have a stable relationship with money GDP. The case for giving more weight to M0 was probably practical rather than theoretical. As figure 4.4 shows, the velocity of circulation of M0 – i.e. the ratio of money GDP to the stock of M0 – had shown a fairly steady trend rise since the 1970s, with no wide short term fluctuations, unlike the velocity of circulation of Sterling M3 which had shown a large rise and fall in the same period. Naturally, the government did not believe that by controlling M0, it could control money GDP; but past behaviour did suggest that M0 was a good *indicator* of money GDP. If, for example, the behaviour of M0 is such as to suggest that, in the judgement, of the policy maker, money GDP is growing at a faster rate than is consistent with a stable or falling inflation rate and realistic output growth, then policy action is required to slow down that growth. The policy action could be a rise in interest rates, aimed not of course at producing a shift of money from non-interest bearing accounts to interest bearing ones – which would simply reflect a change in the velocity of circulation of M0 at a given level of money GDP – but rather at restraining the growth of expenditure on goods and services generally and so slowing the rate of growth of money GDP. However, the policy action need not be 'monetary' – i.e. a rise in interest rates – but could be instead, 'fiscal' – i.e. a cut back in government expenditure or rise in taxation. The choice between monetary and fiscal action would depend on a variety of factors, including the behaviour of and government objectives for the exchange rate.

Clearly, the implication of using M0 as an *indicator* is that policy makers must have an alternative target or objective in mind; so it is not surprising that in budget statements subsequent to 1984, increasing reference was made to the growth of money GDP. Thus in the 1987 budget statement it was said, 'Policy is aimed at maintaining monetary conditions that will bring about a gradual reduction in the growth of money GDP over the medium term'.[21] Accordingly a path for money GDP is laid out, from which the government will 'aim to avoid

20 *Financial Statement and Budget Report, 1987-8*, para 2.17.
21 Ibid., para 2.04.

departures in the medium term'.[22] Emphasis also began to be placed on the exchange rate, partly as an indicator of monetary tightness or ease but also because of its bearing on UK trade competitiveness.

Following its sharp fall in the course of 1981, sterling's effective exchange rate stabilized during 1982. A further sharp fall occurred around the turn of the year; and although there was some correction in the second quarter of 1983, the rate continued to fall through 1984 reaching a low point at the beginning of 1985 (see figure 4.5).

Interpretation of exchange rate movements is no easier than interpretation of monetary aggregates; as always, the problem is to disentangle the various forces operating on it, including external forces such as oil price, as well as dometic monetary conditions. Moreover, interpretation was further complicated by the behaviour of the US dollar which appreciated strongly against all major currencies in the 1981-4 period.[23] Thus, a substantial part of the fall in sterling's effective rate during this period was due to dollar strength rather than sterling weakness. Even so, sterling did decline against the Deutschmark and the yen during this period, suggesting that some weakness existed. Of course, it is possible to point to the acceleration of M0 growth from its low point in the first quarter of 1982, even though Sterling M3 growth had fallen well below its peak of mid 1981. At any rate, the government raised interest rates sharply in January 1985 (see figure 4.6) when the dollar/ sterling rate had fallen to almost 1. But it is also true that oil price was falling through the years 1982-5, eventually plummeting at the end of 1985 and through the first few months of 1986 (figure 4.5). Whatever the relative weights we attach to domestic monetary conditions and oil price fall as causes of sterling's decline through 1983-4, there can be little doubt that oil price was the most important factor in late 1985 and through 1986. Interest rates were raised in October 1986 but the reason for this seemed to lie as much with a sharp rise in M0 growth in the second half of 1986 as in the fall in sterling.

By 1986 the government had come to the conclusion that implementation of monetary policy had to take into account all evidence, including the exchange rate, and not simply the behaviour of the monetary aggregates. Moreover, the government had come to see that there was 'some scope for varying the balance between fiscal and monetary policy, especially in the short run'[24] – a view that eight years previously was probably more acceptable to Keynesians than to monetarists.

22  Ibid., para 2.1.

23  The effective exchange rate of the dollar appreciated by 27% in these years.

24  *Financial Statement and Budget Report, 1986-7*, para 2.06.

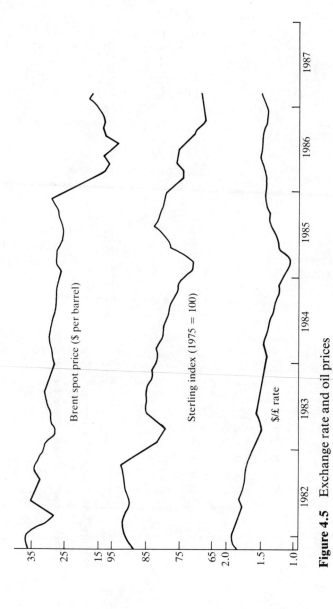

**Figure 4.5** Exchange rate and oil prices

*Source: Financial Statement and Budget Report, 1987–8*

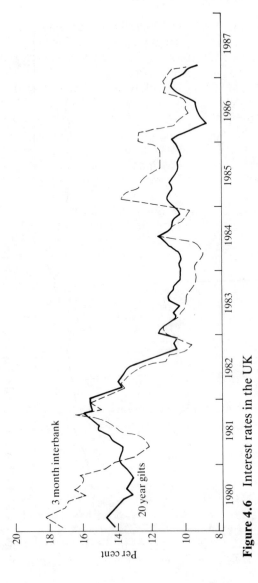

**Figure 4.6** Interest rates in the UK

*Source: Financial Statement and Budget Report, 1987–8*

**The Medium Term Financial Strategy, 1979-87**

This brief survey of the course of the MTFS after 1980 (summarized in earlier tables and in the accompanying figures) indicates that policy was by no means as rigid and unyielding as government rhetoric (or indeed its opponents) suggested. Although in 1987 the government could claim that it had broadly adhered to the fiscal element of its strategy – in the sense that the ratio of the PSBR to GDP in 1986/7 (and projected for 1987/8) was lower than in 1979 – it had clearly departed from it in some of the intervening years. Whether this departure reflected a willingness of the government to pay regard to the so-called cyclical state of the economy, as Professor Walters has suggested,[25] or whether it was *force majeure*, is possibly an open question. In any case, fiscal policy was looser than PSBR targets suggested owing to asset sales. On the other hand, by imposing demands on the capital market, these sales may have kept the monetary situation tighter than was intended. But the government was progressively forced to modify its stance on monetary targeting, so that by 1987 money supply no longer occupied the key role in strategy that it had in 1979–80. The government was no longer 'monetarist' in the sense that it had proudly proclaimed in 1979. This doesn't mean of course that it abandoned monetary policy since interest rates still had (and have) an important role to play.

Although, on the face of it, fiscal and monetary policy in the later years of the MTFS was looser than the government initially intended and constantly affirmed, it nonetheless contained the growth of nominal (money) GDP to less than 10 per cent per annum after 1981 (average 8 per cent per annum 1982–6) as compared with almost 15 per cent per annum through most of the 1970s (see figures 4.1 and 4.2); and this is perhaps the real test. In fact, in the latest year of the strategy, 1986–7, money GDP growth showed a sharp dip to barely 6 per cent per annum compared with over 9 per cent in 1985/6: this hardly suggested that the government had eased up in its long term fight against inflation. No doubt the sharp once-for-all fall in the rate of inflation, which was helped by the steep fall in oil price, contributed to this. But the government clearly thought the decline in money GDP growth was too abrupt, since in the 1987 budget it projected a 7.5 per cent rise in 1987/8, although below 6 per cent remained a long term aim.

25 A. Walters, *Britain's Economic Renaissance* (Oxford University Press, 1986), ch. 5.

Needless to say, although in the eyes of some observers the government had failed to maintain fully the integrity of its strategy as laid down in 1980, others are convinced that policy had remained far too deflationary throughout. Leaving this debate until the next chapter, it will be convenient to finish this one by referring briefly to other elements of the government's strategy before summarizing the impact it had on the economy over these years.

## Privatization and Trade Union Reform

As we have seen, the proceeds of privatization was a significant element in the budgets of 1983 and subsequent years, providing cash flows of over £13 billion to the exchequer (as indicated earlier, these flows entered the budget accounts as negative expenditure), but access to these flows did not, ostensibly at any rate, provide the motivation for privatization *per se*. The government was firmly committed to the view that private ownership and enterprise were superior to public ownership and enterprise, on the grounds of both political philosophy and economic efficiency. The chronic losses of many of Britain's nationalized industries through the post-war period resulted from the 'shadow pricing' (pricing below market price) of the capital and labour resources employed in the industries and therefore could be defended on economic efficiency grounds. Alternatively the losses could be defended by appealing in a Keynesian fashion to the beneficial multiplier effects associated even with activity akin to 'digging holes in the ground'. Even so there was undoubtedly much support from economists and others,[26] not necessarily committed to Tory philosophy or ownership, for action to improve the performance, at any rate in terms of factor productivity, of the country's state owned industries, many of them such as coal and iron and steel, basic to the country's economy. Of course a problem facing the government was that private sector appetite for those industries most in trouble was not likely to be great, at least not until action had been taken to improve their actual and potential performance; so that, in effect, most of the state owned enterprises that were sold in the mid 1980s (see table 4.5) were either in, or about to be in, a profit making position. Thus the government could be and was attacked on grounds that it was selling the nation's profitable assets, a view that not only neglected the possibility that performance could still be improved

26 See R. Pryke, *The Nationalised Industries* (Martin Robertson, Oxford, 1983).

**Table 4.5** Privatizations, 1979–87

| | Date begun | Proceeds (£m) |
|---|---|---|
| British Petroleum | 1979 | 827 |
| National Enterprise Board Holdings | 1979 | 294 |
| British Aerospace | 1981 | 389 |
| North Sea Licences | 1981 | 349 |
| British Sugar Corporation | 1981 | 44 |
| Cables & Wireless | 1981 | 1,024 |
| Amersham International | 1982 | 64 |
| National Freight Consortium | 1982 | 5 |
| Britoil | 1982 | 1,053 |
| Associated British Ports | 1983 | 97 |
| International Aeradio | 1983 | 60 |
| British Rail Hotels | 1983 | 45 |
| Jaguar | 1984 | 297 |
| Sealink | 1984 | 66 |
| Wytch Farm | 1984 | 82 |
| British Telecom | 1984 | 3,682 |
| BT loan stock | 1984 | 158 |
| Enterprise Oil | 1984 | 382 |
| British Shipbuilders Warship Yards | 1985 | 54 |
| British Gas (one-third paid) | 1986 | 5,090 |
| British Airways Helicopters | 1986 | 13 |
| British Gas debt | 1986 | 750 |
| BT preference shares | 1986 | 250 |
| Unipart | 1987 | 52 |
| Leyland Bus | 1987 | 4 |
| Leyland Trucks | 1987 | 0 |
| British Airways (half paid) | 1987 | 825 |
| Royal Ordnance | 1987 | 190 |
| Rolls-Royce (half paid) | 1987 | 1,360 |
| Miscellaneous | 1979–87 | 510 |
| Total | | 18,016 |

under private ownership to the benefit of the consumer, but also contained implicitly within it a Marxian distinction between the nation and the people who comprise it.

The government's attitude to nationalized industries and the public sector provision of services to the community was also conditioned by resentment, which was probably shared by a high proportion of British people in 1979, of the power conferred by so-called public enterprise on public sector trade unions: memories of the 'winter of discontent' were no doubt strong in everyone's mind. Thus, privatization could be seen as one element in a wider policy for improving industrial relations and reducing trade union power. But the government made a more direct attack on this problem, in the form of labour legislation.

Concern at the deleterious impact that poor industrial relations and unbridled union power was having on Britain's economic performance goes back well before the Thatcher government assumed power in 1979, and was shared by many in the Labour party as well as those in the Conservative. Nonetheless, there was reluctance even among Conservatives, and a downright opposition from the trade unions and a majority of the Labour party, to replace the so-called voluntary system that existed by a legislative framework. Moreover, past history seemed to be unpromising.

The Donovan Commission, set up by the Labour government in the mid-1960s, was an early attempt to improve collective bargaining within a voluntary system.[27] An industrial relations commission was suggested which would have the function of scrutinizing collective wage agreements and of making recommendations that hopefully would make the outcome more compatible with national needs; but the Donovan Commission came out very strongly against legislation. In the event, its report was never acted on and its proposals were replaced by the (Labour) government's own White Paper, 'In Place of Strife'. Significantly, this did envisage the use of legal penalties to enforce compliance with government wishes – for example, to enforce acceptance of the recommendations of a commission on industrial relations which it was proposed to set up; however, as a result of trade union opposition, the White Paper was never translated into law.

The Conservative government that came into power in 1970 succeeded in passing an Industrial Relations Act in 1971 which provided for the use of legal penalties to counter so-called 'unfair industrial' practices, and to enforce a 'cooling off' period and a call for strike ballot. An industrial court with a High Court judge as president was set up to deal with the legal issues involved. However, the Act was 'put on ice' in 1972 by the Conservative government that had passed it, in its attempt to get agreement with the trade unions on incomes policy; and it did not last long, being repealed by a new Labour government in

27 Royal Commission on Trade Unions and Employers' Associations, 1965–8, *Report* (CMND 3623, 1968).

1974. Although this Labour government, against a background of acute economic crisis which affected the country through the second half of the 1970s, did succeed in obtaining union co-operation over wage constraint (the so-called 'social contract'), the effect proved divisive; and the unrestrained exercise of power by public sector unions in the 'winter of discontent' eventually contributed to bringing it down.

Thus the Thatcher government came to power against a background of failure of both voluntary and legal attempts to introduce order into British industrial relations and responsibility into wage bargaining. Although apparently committed to not re-introducing the 1971 Industrial Relations Act, the new government was determined on some state intervention in industrial relations. In the course of the next five years, the government introduced three major pieces of legislation.

The first of these was the Employment Act of 1980 introduced by the then Secretary of State for Employment, Mr James Prior. This set out to encourage trade unions to introduce secret ballots on such questions as strike action, amendments to union rules and union elections, by providing government grants to cover the cost. It empowered the Secretary of State to introduce a code of practice on good industrial relations which, although not having the status of a statutory requirement, could be taken into account by tribunals and courts in determining related questions. Various restrictions were introduced relating to the 'closed shop' (for example, new closed shop agreements had to be approved in a secret ballot in which at least 80 per cent of those covered by the agreement supported it; and employees could refuse to join a closed shop on grounds of conscience); restrictions were placed on picketing (picketing was restricted to at or near the work place – moreover, the code of practice mentioned above suggested that a maximum of six pickets was consistent with 'peaceful' picketing); and, very importantly, immunity for secondary industrial action (blacking and sympathetic strikes) was restricted to situations where the main purpose of strike action was to interfere with the production of goods or services of the employer in dispute.

This 'softly-softly' approach favoured by Mr Prior was followed by the bolder approach of his successor, Mr Tebbit, in legislation introduced in 1982. In addition to giving greater protection for non-union members against closed shop practices, and improving the position of non-unionized firms (by making illegal union-enforced discrimination against such firms when contracts were awarded or made, or when industrial action was being taken), the 1982 legislation enabled trade unions as well as trade union officials to be sued for an injunction or damages where they were responsible for 'unlawful action'. It also restricted the definition of a 'lawful trade' dispute, to disputes between workers and their own employer. While much of the effectiveness of the provisions of this 1982 legislation depended on employers being willing to initiate action, the legislation clearly had a potentially strong restraining influence on trade unions in at least two respects: it placed union funds at risk, since unions as well as officials could be sued for damages in their own names if unlawful action had been organized or supported by union officials; and second, because of restrictions on the closed shop, the ability of individual unions to extend unionization was weakened. The 1982 legislation also made political strikes more difficult, with a particular restraining effect on public sector unions, where the distinction between political and industrial strikes could be hard to determine.

The third major piece of legislation, the Trade Union Act of 1984, was aimed at promoting trade union democracy. It sought the election of trade union officials in secret ballots (elections to take place at least once every five years); it laid down that legal immunities in strike action could only be retained if the action was supported by union members in a secret ballot held no more than four weeks before the start of the action; and it laid down that a trade union's ability to maintain a political fund and levy was conditional on a regular ballot of members at least once every ten years. However, a proposal to change the 'contracting out' to a 'contracting in' requirement was not included.

As in the case of previous legislation, the effectiveness of the provision relating to the secret balloting of members no more than four weeks prior to strike action depended on employers being willing to initiate action. However, this seemed increasingly likely in the political and industrial environment ruling in the mid 1980s.

Naturally, the attempt to obtain a legislative framework for industrial relations was met with fierce opposition from unions and the Labour party (although there must have been many who had served in the Labour government in the 1970s who welcomed such legislation). The fact is, however, that Britain was one of the very few industrial countries which had relied almost wholly on a voluntary system of industrial relations, with far from satisfactory results. In the US and most European countries, industrial relations and collective bargaining had a firm legislative base.[28] Thus the Thatcher government's

28 See M.P. Jackson, *Industrial Relations*, 3rd edn (Croom Helmn, 1985).

legislative steps can be seen as no more than a move towards a policy already adopted by other nations.

Undoubtedly such legislation weakened the power of trade unions in Britain, as well as putting pressure on union leaders to behave more responsibly to their members and to the nation; and clearly union power was also weakened, perhaps even more so, by more fundamental forces operating in the economy. Increasing unemployment had reduced the power to enforce wage demands and weakened the willingness of union members to go on strike. The irreversible decline in Britain's basic 'smokestack' industries, which were large employers of labour, had greatly reduced trade union membership; and trade unions were slow, and indeed may have found it difficult, to recruit members in new high technology and service based industries which tended to grow fast, often in new 'green field' areas of the country. Finally, one must not overlook the importance of the government's own attitude towards strikes. Its unwillingness to concede to strike pressure, even when supported by considerable physical violence on the picket lines as in the 12 months long coal-miners' strike of 1984–5, headed by Mr Scargill, helped create a psychological climate in which union leaders were forced to recognize that they could no longer exercise the political and economic power that they did in the 1970s. Indeed, there can be little doubt that the government's defeat of that strike – which owed nothing to industrial legislation *per se* – had a greater impact on industrial relations than legislation itself.

## Macroeconomic Results

What then were the results of the Thatcher strategy as pursued from 1979 to 1987 in terms of the conventional macroeconomic variables such as output, employment, inflation, balance of payments and so on (reference to what might be regarded as deeper, more fundamental results will be left to chapter 7). Table 4.6 provides a summary.

Clearly, looking at the period 1979–87 as a whole, we have a very mixed picture. Looking at it from the output and employment side, the results appear to range from poor to disastrous. Real GDP has risen by about 18 per cent (2.0 per cent per annum), and industrial production by about 5.5 per cent whilst manufacturing production has barely changed.[29] By 1983 the UK had a deficit in manufactures in its trade with

29 Manufacturing production in the third quarter of 1987 exceeded that of 1979.

**Table 4.6** Macroeconomic performance in the Thatcher period

|  | Output | | | Employment (1980 = 100) | | |
|---|---|---|---|---|---|---|
|  | GDP *(1980 prices)* | Industrial production *(1980 prices)* | Manu- facturing output *(1980 prices)* | Total civil | Industrial production | Manu- facturing |
| 1970 | 99.8 | 103.2 | 109.7 | 100.1 | 104.8 | 106.8 |
| 1970 | 102.4 | 107.1 | 109.5 | 101.7 | 105.0 | 106.3 |
| 1980 | 100.0 | 100.0 | 100.0 | 100.9 | 101.4 | 101.6 |
| 1981 | 98.7 | 96.6 | 94.0 | 96.1 | 91.8 | 91.1 |
| 1982 | 100.3 | 98.4 | 94.2 | 94.0 | 86.7 | 85.9 |
| 1983 | 103.8 | 101.9 | 96.9 | 92.5 | 82.2 | 81.0 |
| 1984 | 106.7 | 103.2 | 100.7 | 93.3 | 80.5 | 79.2 |
| 1985 | 110.5 | 108.2 | 103.9 | 94.4 | 79.5 | 78.6 |
| 1986 | 113.6 | 110.0 | 104.0 | 94.8 | 77.2 | 76.8 |
| 1987[a] | (118.4) | (113.0) | (109.5) | 96.0 | 75.8 | 75.4 |
|  | % change | % change | % change | % change | % change | % change |
| 1979–87 | +15.7 | +5.5 | +0.0 | −5.7 | −27.8 | −29.0 |
| 1979–81 | −3.6 | −9.9 | −14.2 | −5.5 | −13.2 | −13.3 |
| 1981–7 | +20.0 | +16.9 | +16.5 | 0 | −17.5 | −16.8 |

[a] Estimated.
[b] Not comparable with earlier years owing to revision of basis of calculation.
*Sources*: OECD and National Institute of Economic and Social Research

the rest of the world, a fact which caused particular consternation among politicians and businessmen, and even among some economists, though Britain's newly acquired status as a substantial oil producer and exporter almost certainly implied a decline in net exports of manufactures. Total civilian employment fell by 6 per cent whilst employment in production industries, including manufacturing, fell by 28 per cent. Unemployment increased by almost 2 million and, as a proportion of the labour force, rose from less than 5 per cent to (at one time) over 12.5 per cent. On the other hand, inflation came down markedly, from an average of 13.5 per cent in 1979 (and a peak rate of nearly 20 per cent at the end of that year) to an average of 3 per cent in

| Unemployment | | Productivity (1980 = 100) | | Inflation Rate | Balance of Payments (£ million) |
|---|---|---|---|---|---|
| (thousands) | % of labour force | Whole economy | Manu-facturing | % change in retail price | Current account |
| 1,225.0 | 5.1 | 100.2 | 103.4 | 8.3 | + 965 |
| 1,140.5 | 4.7 | 102.1 | 104.0 | 13.5 | − 496 |
| 1,451.7 | 6.0 | 100.0 | 100.0 | 17.9 | +3,122 |
| 2,269.8 | 9.4 | 102.0 | 103.5 | 11.9 | +6,936 |
| 2,626.1 | 10.9 | 105.9 | 109.7 | 8.6 | +4,685 |
| 2,866.0 | 11.9 | 110.0 | 117.9 | 4.6 | +3,832 |
| 2,998.3 | 12.4 | 111.7 | 123.4 | 5.0 | +2,022 |
| 3,113,1 | 12.9 | 114.1 | 127.0 | 6.1 | +3,387 |
| 3,180.0 | 11.5[b] | 117.0 | 134.8 | 3.4 | − 175 |
| (2,880.8) | 10.2 | (120.3) | (142.7) | 4.1 | +2,687 |
| | | % change | % change | | |
| | | +17.8 | +37.2 | | |
| | | − 0.1 | − 0.5 | | |
| | | +17.9 | +37.8 | | |

1986; and productivity of labour rose substantially, particularly in manufacturing (by nearly 40 per cent) and production industries generally, and at a significantly higher rate than for most of the post-war period. The current account of the balance of payments was in surplus until 1986, and the country acquired overseas assets on a substantial scale. Real personal disposable income rose by more than 10 per cent and real consumption expenditure by even more (13 per cent). Real fixed investment expenditure also rose (by 5.5 per cent), though it fell as a proportion of GDP.

Although fixed investment in plant and machinery rose substantially (by 15 per cent), this seems to have been carried out more in distribution and financial and business services than in production industries, since fixed investment in manufacturing industry declined. Residential investment also fell.

A somewhat different light is thrown on these developments if we break the whole period into two parts: 1979–81 and 1981–7. Output fell substantially in the first sub-period, but rose strongly in the second. Employment fell in both sub-periods before turning up in 1984, whilst unemployment rose to a peak in 1986 before falling sharply through 1987. As a consequence, productivity rose substantially in the second sub-period, having been rather flat in the first. Inflation continued to decline throughout. In isolation, therefore, 1981–7 presents a more than satisfactory picture, except for the high level of unemployment remaining at the end of 1987.[30]

Success with inflation but failure on unemployment complicates the task of assessment, as does the contrast between the two sub-periods. Was the pick-up in output growth in the period 1981–7 merely a belated and insufficient turn round from the steep recession in 1979–81 or was it in fact conditioned by it? Was Britain's greatly improved productivity performance after 1981 dependent on structural and other changes that were forced on the economy in 1979–81? Although the decline in inflation was desirable, indeed necessary, could it have been achieved with less fall in employment, and better manufacturing performance in terms of output? How far was British government policy responsible for the good and bad features of developments in 1979–87? What was the contribution of North Sea oil and other external developments? An attempt at answering some of these questions is contained in later chapters.

No other period in post Second World War years has aroused so much controversy among economists and politicians as has the Thatcher period. Indeed for a large proportion of the economics profession, if not a majority of it, hostility is a more apt term than controversy. The next two chapters review some of the criticisms of the Thatcher strategy and its implementation, and the final chapter attempts an overall assessment.

---

30 Unemployment fell by another half million in 1988.

# 5

# The Strategy Criticized (1): Monetary and Fiscal Policy

It is hardly surprising that a strategy which is associated with a two-and-a-half fold rise in unemployment in a period of barely six years attracted a great deal of criticism and political opposition. The government has also been accused of pursuing policies that have 'destroyed' manufacturing industry, resulting in the country becoming dependent on net imports of manufactures for the first time since the industrial revolution. It is also charged with the wasting of North Sea oil revenue which, according to critics, has either been splurged on a consumer boom or invested abroad instead of at home, to the long term competitive disadvantage of British industry. If this is all true, the government could be indicted for virtual treason against the British people.

The criticism is particularly strong from those economists who regard the maintenance of full employment as the most important objective for policy, apparently regardless of the inflation that might accompany it; but severe criticism also comes from others giving equal recognition to the evil of inflation as well as unemployment, but who believe that intervention of one kind or another in wage bargaining and wage determination would have enabled the very necessary fall in inflation to be combined with less fall in employment. In general, all these economists believe that the abandonment of Keynesian demand management was a mistake, as was the adoption of so-called 'monetarism'. On the other hand, there are other economists, although no doubt fewer in number, who maintain that fiscal and monetary tightness has not been carried far enough; and there are still others with overlapping views who, far from believing that the government should have intervened in the wage setting process, hold that it should have moved to make labour markets much more competitive by abolishing collective bargaining, thereby further reducing the monopolistic power of the trade unions.

This chapter and the next will consider some of these criticisms, leaving until the final chapter an overall assessment of the strategy pursued. However, it may be useful to begin here with a brief review of the experience of some other major industrial countries in this period, to see how far that experience differed from or was similar to the experience of the UK. A comparison of this kind may help to place UK policy and performance in better perspective.

## How Other Countries Fared

Table 5.1 summarizes the behaviour of some of the relevant macro-economic variables of the major industrial countries of the OECD. A number of comparisons stand out. First and most obvious, is the greatly superior performance of Japan and (to a lesser extent) the US in terms of output and employment over that of the European countries. Second, within the European group, the performance of the UK over the whole period 1979–87 has not been significantly different from that of the other three major countries, although clearly Germany looks somewhat better if weight is given to industrial production and inflation.

Third, and perhaps significantly, the UK did better in terms of GDP and output growth after 1981 than did the other three European countries, including Germany, and indeed not greatly less well than the US; and although unemployment was always at a higher level, it appears to have increased somewhat less quickly than in Germany and France. Thus, if the Thatcher strategy is held to be primarily responsible for the relatively depressed economic state of the UK economy, it certainly seems to have been matched in other major European countries.[1]

It is clear from table 5.1 that the main difference between the UK's economic performance and that of the other European countries is that the UK plunged somewhat earlier and more deeply into the recession which afflicted all industrial countries following the second oil price shock of 1979-80.

While GDP and industrial production were generally maintained in the rest of Europe they fell sharply in the UK. Unemployment in the

---

1 Most of the smaller European countries did no better and some of them, for example Belgium, Netherlands, Denmark and Spain, had worse unemployment records. See *Economic Outlook* OECD, May 1986.

**Table 5.1** Macroeconomic performances by major industrial countries, 1979–87

| Variables | UK | Germany | France | Italy | US | Japan |
|---|---|---|---|---|---|---|
| **Change in GDP (%)** | | | | | | |
| 1979–87 | +16.4 | +12.1 | +14.2 | +19.9 | +20.4 | +35.4 |
| 1979–81 | −3.6 | +1.5 | +2.8 | +5.1 | +1.6 | +8.0 |
| 1981–7 | +20.4 | +10.6 | +11.0 | +11.1 | +18.4 | +25.2 |
| **Change in industrial production (%)** | | | | | | |
| 1979–87 | +8.8 | +8.0 | +2.0 | +9.4 | +16.9 | +30.0 |
| 1979–81 | −9.4 | −1.0 | −1.0 | +3.0 | 0 | +5.0 |
| 1981–7 | +12.1 | +9.0 | +3.0 | +11.6 | +16.9 | +28.9 |
| **Unemployment as % of labour force** | | | | | | |
| 1979 | 5.0 | 3.2 | 5.9 | 7.6 | 5.8 | 2.1 |
| 1981 | 9.8 | 4.4 | 7.3 | 8.3 | 7.5 | 2.2 |
| 1987 | 10.6 | 6.3 | 10.6 | 11.0[a] | 6.1 | 2.8 |
| **Inflation (% per annum)** | | | | | | |
| 1979 | 13.4 | 4.1 | 10.8 | 14.8 | 11.3 | 3.6 |
| 1987 | 4.1 | 0.1 | 2.2 | 4.7 | 3.7 | 0.0 |
| **Increase in labour productivity in manufacturing (% per annum)** | | | | | | |
| 1979–86 | 3.8 | 2.6 | 2.8 | 2.7 | 3.9 | 2.6 |
| 1981–6 | 4.7 | 3.3 | 3.5 | 2.2 | 4.4 | 3.0 |

[a] 1986

*Source: National Institute Economic Review* and *OECD Economic Outlook*

UK doubled against smaller but still substantial increases in the other countries. Thus, if *particular* criticism is to be directed at the Thatcher administration – separate from criticism that might be directed at macroeconomic policy pursued in Europe as a whole (and possibly at policy pursued by the US as well, although from a different point of view)[2] – it has to be focused on policy pursued in the first two years, 1979–81, of that administration.

A complicating factor immediately arises since, as we have noted in an earlier chapter, the oil price rise of 1979–80 coincided with the UK becoming a substantial oil producer. Although the assumption of oil producer status at a time of massive price rise was obviously of major benefit to the UK economy overall, it had a structural impact on the UK economy which distinguished the impact of the oil price rise on the UK from that on the mainly oil-importing European economies. This has to be borne in mind when assessing macroeconomic policy *per se*. Indeed, examination of that structural impact suggests that at least one of the charges against that policy – namely the charge that government policy had reduced the UK to the lowly and ignominious status of a net importer of manufactures for the first time in 200 years – is misleading if not actually irrelevant. It ignores the fact that the UK became a substantial net exporter of oil, for the first time ever.

In 1979, the UK was a net importer of mineral fuels, largely oil, by around £1.8 billion (a little less than 1 per cent of GDP); by 1985, it had become a net exporter of these products by just over £6 billion (2 per cent of GDP). Evidently, the UK had less *need* to export manufactures to pay for oil in 1985 than in 1979. In relation to GDP, the turnround in the trade position in fuels amounted to 2.9 per cent of GDP. Since the UK's net exports of manufactures (including chemicals) in 1979 amounted to only 1.5 per cent of GDP, a decline in net exports of manufactures of similar size to the improvement in the UK's net position in fuels would have pushed the UK into a deficit in manufactures of about 1.4 per cent of GDP. Thus, in a structural sense, the appearance of a manufacturing deficit should not have been entirely unexpected.[3]

But although not 'unexpected', a deficit in manufactures was not logically necessary. In principle the turnround in the UK's net trading position in fuels could have been absorbed by an equivalent improve-

---

2 Perhaps more by accident than design, expansionary fiscal policy pulled the US out of its recession of 1980–2, but at the expense of a massive deficit in the current account of its balance of payments which seems certain to constrain future growth.

3 The UK also became less dependent on food imports in this period, reflecting the boost given to British farming by entrance into the EEC and the Common Agricultural Policy. Indeed by 1987 Britain had become the world's seventh largest food producer, a fact which does not necessarily accord with the best distribution of the country's resources.

ment in the UK's current account balance of payments position with the rest of the world, leaving the manufacturing surplus unaffected. Professor Kaldor was a leading critic of the government for not pursuing the exchange rate policy, i.e. a much lower nominal sterling exchange rate, that would have produced this result.[4] In fact, the UK's current account position with the rest of the world did improve significantly after 1979, from a small deficit (0.35 per cent of GDP in that year), to a surplus of over 1.5 per cent of GDP in 1985 (in 1981, the surplus was closer to 2 per cent of GDP). In effect, the UK invested overseas about 40 per cent of the gain produced by North Sea oil for its trade position in fuels (see chapter 3 for a further discussion of this point), a fact which did not escape criticism from those believing that North Sea oil revenue should have been invested at home rather than overseas – some of whom, somewhat inconsistently, also blamed the government for policies that produced the manufacturing deficit (i.e. for allowing *insufficient* investment overseas). Whether or not the UK could have improved its current account balance of payments position more than it did – thus reducing the impact of North Sea oil on its net trading position in manufactures – must remain in doubt. It would have been difficult to maintain the UK's net manufacturing surplus during a period when other major *oil-importing* countries were taking restrictive monetary and fiscal measures aimed at containing the balance of payments and inflationary consequences of the 1979–80 oil price shock.

These countries were under pressure to increase their net exports of manufactures to pay for higher cost oil, quite unlike the UK whose trade position had benefited from higher oil price. It is certain that the attempt to get export-led growth on the basis of nominal sterling depreciation would have required a willingness of the UK labour force to accept a decline in the product real wage, a willingness that was not likely to have been forthcoming at the time. Moreover sterling depreciation would have exacerbated an already serious inflationary situation.

But while a manufacturing *deficit* of some proportion was probably inevitable, it does not follow that UK manufacturing output and GDP had to fall as much as they did in the course of 1979–81. In principle, expansionary policies could have been pursued that would have been consistent with a manufacturing deficit at a higher level of imports and output (and possibly exports as well). Thus dismissal of the charge that policy caused a manufacturing deficit does not absolve the government

4 See his letter to the *Financial Times*, 13 Feb. 1986.

from the charge of pursuing monetary and fiscal policies that were too restrictive.

As indicated in earlier chapters, the government linked monetary and fiscal policy together in a Medium Term Financial Strategy. This practice itself was open to criticism since it appeared to subordinate fiscal policy to monetary policy, thereby eliminating, or at any rate weakening, the role fiscal policy could have played in maintaining employment, even in the context of an anti-inflationary monetary policy. However, we shall discuss monetary and fiscal policy separately, beginning with the former. Policy with regard to employment is left to the next chapter.

## Monetary Policy

It is evident from the behaviour of the monetary aggregates discussed in the previous chapter that in so far as monetary policy is concerned, the force of the criticism of tightness applies more to the 1979–81 period than to the years after: emphasis on money supply control was progressively modified in later years; and by 1985/6 effective monetary targeting (apart from M0) was virtually abandoned. Even in 1979–81, money supply targets set by the government (7–11 per cent Sterling M3 growth in each of 1979/80 and 1980/81) did not suggest that the government was aiming for 'shock' treatment rather than 'gradualism', although 'shock' treatment seemed to be the result. In retrospect, in setting targets for monetary growth the government can be criticized for ignoring autonomous cost and price raising pressures that were either already built into the system, as a result of policies pursued by the previous administration, or had been introduced by itself (the VAT increase, for example, or the Clegg pay award implementation). Also it may have underestimated the impact on domestic monetary conditions of the decision to abolish foreign exchange control (an otherwise correct decision in the light of the impact of North Sea oil and the long term need to raise the productivity of capital at home). However, the main failure lay in an initial misinterpretation of the behaviour of Sterling M3, which failed to respond in the expected way to rising interest rates.

It may be recalled from discussion in chapter 2 that a rise in interest rates could be expected to impact on Sterling M3 growth through broadly two channels: first, by reducing the demand for commercial bank loans; and second, by causing depositors to reduce their holding of money balances, in favour of interest bearing bonds or similar assets. In other words, both the demand for money (i.e. bank deposits) and the demand for bank credit are expected to be normally elastic with respect to the rate of interest. In the circumstances of 1979–80, bank lending did not respond in the expected way to the rise in bank lending rates; on the contrary, in an attempt to stay alive in the recession that soon engulfed them, firms were forced into 'distress borrowing' from banks. Thus bank lending rose as interest rates rose, rather than fell. Of course, this could not be a long term solution for firms in difficulties. If there were no change in the situation, bank-ruptcies would soon follow and bank lending would be reduced; in the long run, the normal relationship between interest rates and borrowing would be restored. In the short run, however, bank lending and loan interest rates can be perversely related, and appeared to be so in 1979–80.

However, banks cannot increase their lending unless they can increase their deposits; and this is the area in which most problems arose for the government in its determination to control Sterling M3.

The first problem, which assumed particular significance in 1979–81, is the impact of rising interest rates on international capital movements. Money is attracted from other international financial centres by the prospect of higher returns: other things being equal, inflows of foreign capital would tend to swell UK money supply. However, the problem lies less in the potential impact of capital inflows on bank deposits and money supply than in the policy choice forced on the central bank, in this case the Bank of England. The Bank can certainly prevent or restrain domestic money creation by refraining from intervention in the foreign exchange market, i.e. by being unwilling to provide sterling in exchange for the foreign currency being offered. When this happens, the exchange rate appreciates either in association with an increase in money supply or instead of it, depending on the resolve of the Bank.

Of course, it is important to note that the attraction of high interest rates in the UK for foreign funds will be qualified by the exchange rate risk faced by foreign investors when buying sterling. If sterling should fall in value subsequent to the purchase, the foreign investor will find that some of the gain that he expected to get from higher interest rates in the UK will be lost; indeed, he could end up by making no gain at all and even a loss. Thus if sterling is viewed as a risky currency, interest rates have to be that much higher in the UK than elsewhere to persuade foreign investors to move in. Conceivably there could be no interest rate differential that was sufficiently attractive, in which case the choice between sterling appreciation and rising domestic money supply would not be faced by the UK monetary authorities. The money supply target would then be achieved by a level of interest rates that would eventually constrain bank lending. If that happened, however, the domestic monetary squeeze being imposed by the government would be more widely spread and its impact less concentrated on the export and import-competing sectors of the economy.

In the circumstances of 1979–80, when North Sea oil came on stream and world oil price rose, sterling probably appeared a less risky currency than most others. The so-called 'Thatcher effect' may also have played an important role. Given external confidence in sterling, high interest rates in the UK proved a strong inducement to external money inflow during these years.[5] Thus the government's determination to pull Sterling M3 growth into its target range inevitably meant strong upward pressure on the exchange rate, quite apart from pressure that came from the UK's newly assumed oil price status. Even so, Sterling M3 targets were exceeded in 1979 and 1980.

Although no doubt convinced of the need to restrict monetary growth if inflation was to be pulled down, and of the key role to be played by the exchange rate in the process, the government was undoubtedly surprised (and possibly dismayed) by the speed and magnitude of sterling's rise. The attempt to pull Sterling M3 into its target range by raising interest rates was soon abandoned; indeed, the government's learning time in this respect was much shorter than critics have given credit for. In any case, Sterling M3 growth rate came down in 1981 and 1982; and since target ranges were also raised, the problem of excess money growth seemed to have passed. But Sterling M3 growth did not remain 'well behaved' for long. Growth began to accelerate in mid 1984, and by 1986/7 Sterling M3 was rising as fast as in 1980/1 (see figure 4.2).

However, the problem did not lie in capital inflows, as in 1979–81: interest rates were substantially lower through 1984–6, and the exchange rate was generally falling throughout (figures 4.5 and 4.6). The problem now lay in the structural change and financial innovation that was taking place at a rapid rate in the UK financial system.

The key development in this period which complicated Sterling M3 control was the rapidly growing competition of the commercial banks for deposit and lending business. In the 1960s and the 1970s, the

5 The 'confidence effect' associated with the UK's newly assumed oil producer status is probably a further reason for giving more weight than some economists are prepared to concede to the impact of North Sea oil on the UK's exchange rate during these years. (The more important reasons are discussed in chapter 3).

commercial banks had lost out against other financial institutions, in particular the building societies, partly because of inbred conservatism but also because of regulatory controls which restrained bank lending either directly or indirectly by constraining the growth of deposits. With the abolition of the 'corset' (i.e. the regulation governing the amount of interest bearing eligible liabilities that commercial banks could hold) in 1980 the banks were able to compete more actively for deposits. No doubt attitudes had also changed, so that the banks became more aggressive in offering new products on both the liability and asset sides of their balance sheet. Interest bearing deposits expanded rapidly in the 1980s,[6] and the distinction between transaction balances and investment balances became increasingly blurred, as interest was offered on chequable accounts as well as on the more usual deposit accounts.[7] Sterling M3 became a less and less accurate measure of 'money' in the normal sense. Moreover, the growth of Sterling M3 became dependent not only on the growth of financial intermediation in the economy as a whole but also on the commercial banks' share, which was also rising. Since financial intermediation was growing at a faster rate than the economy as a whole, Sterling M3 increased at a faster rate than money GDP; and its velocity of circulation fell, despite high and stable interest rates (figure 4.4).

This structural development did not mean that Sterling M3 could not be controlled although, with more and more bank deposits earning interest, the relevant control measure became the *differential* between the interest rate on deposits and the interest rate on public sector debt, rather than the level of interest rates *per se*. The public sector debt interest rate would have to rise relatively to the bank deposit rate to persuade bank depositors to shift out of their balances into government bonds. In fact, in the years after 1984, interbank rates generally remained above the bond rate, providing no incentive for balances to be shifted (figure 4.6). A sufficient rise in interest rates generally would no doubt eventually bring Sterling M3 under control ultimately through its impact on bank lending, but once against this would be at the expense of an appreciating exchange rate and a return to the condition of 1979–81. In other words, control over Sterling M3 could certainly be achieved, but only at an unacceptable cost in terms of interest

6 By the mid 1980s, interest bearing deposits represented about three-quarters of Sterling M3 as against less than 60% in the early 1970s.

7 Interest bearing sterling sight deposits rose almost threefold between the end of 1982 and the end of 1986.

rates and the exchange rate. The government had learned from its previous experience and clearly did not wish to repeat it.

Nonetheless there are still those who believe that abandonment of control over Sterling M3 was a mistake and that the danger of a possible return to the high inflation rates of the 1970s hangs over the economy. This would certainly be the case if the previous relationship between Sterling M3, interest rates and money GDP were restored. Given the present stock of Sterling M3, a substantial rise in money GDP and in the price level would be inevitable; but this seems unlikely, and indeed the argument overlooks osme important factors.[8] First, Sterling M3 expansion has not resulted from relaxation of monetary policy *per se*: nominal and real interest remained high through 1984-6 and although (at the time of writing) the exchange rate is well below the levels of 1979-81 (which can be explained at least in part by weakening oil price), it cannot be said to be weak. Second, there has clearly been a substantial increase in the demand for money (i.e. Sterling M3) as well as in the supply. This is in part due to the fact that financial innovation has provided investors with an interest bearing, capital safe asset which has advantages over capital uncertain assets such as bonds, and part due to a structural change in deposit ownership. Owing to the payments mechanism provided by the commercial banks, other (non-bank) financial institutions have accumulated monetary claims on banks as their own business has expanded. The accumulation of such balances does not represent potential demand for goods and services.

In essence, the UK financial system has undergone a stock adjustment process in which investors have radically shifted the composition of their portfolios in response to changes in relative returns. During this process, the 'normal' relationship between changes in the velocity of circulation of Sterling M3 and changes in the rate of interest has been distorted: the ratio of money Sterling M3 to money GDP has risen without a fall in interest rates being necessary. With the ending of the stock adjustment process, we may well see a return to the more normal positive relationship between the two; but it seems unlikely that, at a given rate of interest, the ratio of money to money GDP will fall to earlier levels. For this reason, we may perhaps discount the latent inflationary threat apparently imposed by the build-up of Sterling M3.

Could the government have anticipated the problems associated with interpreting and controlling the behaviour of Sterling M3, hence avoiding the 1979-81 'shock' treatment of the British economy? Leaving until the final chapter the question whether 'shock' treatment was in fact the wrong policy given the nature of the long term problems

8 In retrospect, this conclusion may seem to be somewhat complacent. In 1987 and 1988 money GDP growth and the rate of inflation accelerated sharply.

affecting the British economy, the answer must be 'yes' since, in principle, the relationship between money supply, interest rates and the exchange rate in a floating exchange rate system was certainly well known before 1979.

Nonetheless, the complexity and magnitude of the forces operating on Sterling M3, on the exchange rate, and on the economy in general in 1979–81 – namely North Sea oil, oil price rise, incipient and actual world recession – would in practice have been difficult to assess. In fact monetarists did not provide much guidance in the period, and only after the event did they indicate the unreliability of Sterling M3 as an indicator of monetary tightness and ease, and of the consequent need to pay more attention to narrow money such as M1 and M0. Moreover the pace of technological and structural change in the UK financial system in the 1980s must have surprised practitioners as much as the government. Clearly, developments of this nature cannot be and should not be restrained by monetary policy, and as we have seen the government did not attempt to do so. [9]

Non-monetarists can of course claim that they would not have embarked on the monetarist strategy in the first place, but given the failure of alternative means of controlling inflation – the collapse of incomes policy in 1978 can hardly be overlooked – it is not clear how the inflationary pressures building up in the economy in 1978 could have been handled. In the absence of a reasonably clear policy on money supply, a particular danger would have been an attempt to prevent any real appreciation of sterling through 1979–80. Given North Sea oil and the further massive rise in oil price in 1979–80, some real appreciation of sterling was inevitable, and an attempt to prevent it by unrestrained monetary expansion would have produced massive inflation in the UK and a return to the situation of the 1970s. Real appreciation would not have been avoided but would have been produced by faster domestic inflation rather than by a rise in the nominal exchange rate.

In view of what has been said about the difficulty of controlling Sterling M3 except at unacceptable cost in terms of interest rates and the exchange rate, there also has to be reservation about the argument

---

9 It could be argued that as a result of these innovations, the UK financial system is becoming closer to that described in the Radcliffe Report. But whereas the Radcliffe Committee believed that short run macro-control of the economy should be exercised through fiscal policy with interest rates being set at a level that would balance investment and saving in the long run, the current policy view seems to be the opposite; namely that policy should aim at fiscal balance in the long run, whilst short term control is exerted through interest rates.

that the introduction of the MTFS led to fiscal policy being unnecessarily subordinated to monetary policy, so weakening any role that fiscal policy could have played, even within the context of a restrictive monetary policy. Indeed the opposite can be argued, since if monetary policy cannot be effectively applied except at high cost in terms of interest rates and the exchange rate – which seems to be the lesson of the 1980s – then more, not less, onus is thrown on fiscal policy for controlling aggregate demand and inflation. Nonetheless, the view is widely held that fiscal policy was unnecessarily restrictive, not simply in 1979–81 when monetary squeeze and real exchange rate appreciation were the dominant factors affecting the economy, but also in subsequent years when monetary squeeze had been greatly eased and sterling's real exchange rate was substantially lower. Hence, in the next section we turn to criticism of fiscal policy *per se*.

## Fiscal Policy

As measured by the PSBR, fiscal policy appeared to have been expansionary throughout the Thatcher years. Government expenditure exceeded tax revenue (plus the proceeds of asset sales) in every year of the MTFS. In Keynesian terms there was a net injection of purchasing power averaging some 4 per cent of GDP (in terms of the public sector financial deficit) (table 4.3). However, the nominal budget surplus or deficit is not a good indicator of fiscal stance and has to be adjusted in at least two respects if a truer indication of that stance is to be obtained.

The need for the first adjustment arises from the fact that some components of both expenditure and tax revenue are a function of the level of economic activity as well as a determinant of it. Policy may set tax rates and also some levels of government expenditure, but the amount of tax revenue that is actually collected and the amount that the government actually spends *ex post* will be determined by what happens to national income and employment. The relationship is obvious in the case of tax revenue since, although tax *rates* may be set by the Treasury, the amount of revenue actually raised will depend on the level of incomes that actually materialize in the fiscal period; and this could be higher or lower than the government anticipated at the time of the budget. The same may be true of expenditure, since many items of expenditure, for example social security benefits such as unemployment pay, are closely related to what happens to income and employment. Hence, although a balancing of expenditure and tax revenue may be planned, a deficit or surplus may result if the country's national income is smaller or greater than was anticipated. A budget deficit which appears *ex post*, for example, is therefore not a reliable indication that fiscal policy was expansionary in the fiscal period. On the contrary, it could have been contractionary *ex ante*, thereby producing the fall in incomes that caused the deficit.

The need for a so-called 'cyclical adjustment' to the actual budget surplus or deficit figures is therefore generally accepted for an assessment of how loose or tight fiscal policy has been in the period in question. Given a situation of apparent unemployment of labour and other resources, a typical approach is to assess what government expenditure and tax revenue would have been if the economy had been fully employed, on the basis of given tax and social security benefit rates and autonomous expenditure not related to the level of income. Of course a major problem is the assessment of potential full employment output and its associated national income level, and a typical approach is to apply a capacity output growth rate, based on past performance, to a base year in which resources seem to have been fully employed. Since past performance is no guarantee of future performance, particularly if the economy is faced with big shifts in relative prices and is engaged in structural shifts in resources (as was the case in the 1970s and for different reasons in the 1980s), the danger in such an approach is obvious, so that great care must be taken in drawing conclusions about fiscal stance.

It is also contended that actual budget deficit or surplus figures should be adjusted for inflation, which imposes an implicit tax on the private sector. This arises because the outstanding monetary liability of the public sector – i.e. the cumulative value of the debt instruments issued by the public sector to finance past deficits – is eroded by inflation. Since this public sector liability is also the asset of the private sector, this latter sector is in effect being subjected to an inflation tax, the implicit revenue from which is not included in current government revenue. Thus there is a case for adding this inflation tax to government revenue when assessing the stance of fiscal policy. Of course, the interest rate the government has to pay on its borrowing from the private sector is not unaffected by inflation: nominal interest rates and the interest burden on public sector debt is likely to rise with inflation. Even so, whereas interest payments on public sector debt is included in public sector expenditure, the implicit inflation tax on public sector monetary liabilities is not.

Table 5.2, taken from Miller,[10] provides estimates of cyclical and inflation adjustments that should be applied to the Public Sector Financial Balance (PSFB), and the resulting adjusted structural balance as per cent of GDP (line 5) for the period 1970-1984 (the Public Sector Financial Balance rather than the PSBR is used here since, by excluding income from Public Sector asset sales, it provides a better indication of fiscal stance: see Chapter 4).

It will be seen that whereas on an unadjusted basis the PSFB was in deficit for all of the years 1979-84 (indicating fiscal expansion), on an adjusted basis it was in substantial surplus (indicating fiscal contraction). It is noteworthy however that this apparent contradiction applied also throughout the 1970s: the unadjusted balance indicates fiscal expansion; the adjusted balance indicates contraction. The suggestion that fiscal policy was contractionary during the 1970s when inflation averaged 14 per cent per annum is no doubt surprising and will be received with some scepticism; but the explanation lies partly in inflation itself (see line 4) and partly in the fact that real interest rates were negative throughout most of the 1970s (compare lines 3 and 4 of table 5.3): nominal interest rates failed to adjust upwards with the inflation rate. Since it is unlikely that the government could finance itself on a long term basis at negative real interest rates (the fact that it was able to do so in the 1970s arose from the failure of investors in government debt to anticipate the very rapid rise in inflation that took place), Professor Miller has suggested that a truer picture of the real cost of government debt service would be obtained if a long term real interest rate (say 2.5 per cent) were applied to the market value of debt.[11] If this were done, a 'truer' picture of the inflation-adjusted structural balance would also be obtained; and it would then appear that the adjusted structural balance was in deficit throughout the 1970s, a result perhaps somewhat more acceptable to common sense. Certainly, a sceptical observer would have to be convinced that the very large *unadjusted* public sector deficits averaging over 5 per cent of GDP during that second half of the decade had no causal connection with the inflation of those years or that the much smaller *unadjusted* deficits of 1980-4, averaging less than 4 per cent of GDP, had little or nothing to do with the decline in inflation.

More convincing perhaps is the need for cyclical correction for, as

10 M. Miller, 'Measuring the stance of fiscal policy', *Oxford Review of Economic Policy*, 1 (Spring 1985).

11 Ibid. The paper contains an interesting discussion of the problem of measuring interest rates in times of inflation.

**Table 5.2** Cyclical and inflation adjusting the public sector financial balance: UK 1970–84 (% GDP)

| | 1970 | 1971 | 1972 | 1973 | 1974 | 1975 | 1976 | 1977 | 1978 | 1979 | 1980 | 1981 | 1982 | 1983 | 1984 |
|---|---|---|---|---|---|---|---|---|---|---|---|---|---|---|---|
| 1. Public sector financial balance | 1.3 | – 0.5 | – 2.5 | – 3.8 | – 5.7 | – 7.2 | – 6.7 | – 4.2 | – 4.9 | – 4.4 | – 4.9 | – 3.6 | – 2.8 | – 3.6 | – 4.3 |
| 2. Cyclical correction | 0 | 0.1 | 0.4 | – 1.0 | 0 | 1.3 | 1.5 | 1.4 | 0.4 | 0 | 2.4 | 4.6 | 5.4 | 5.3 | 4.8 |
| 3. Structural balance | 1.3 | – 0.4 | – 2.1 | – 4.8 | – 5.7 | – 5.9 | – 5.2 | – 2.8 | – 4.5 | – 4.4 | – 2.5 | 1.0 | 2.6 | 1.7 | 0.5 |
| 4. 'Current' inflation adjustment | 5.2 | 5.5 | 4.8 | 5.4 | 11.1 | 11.2 | 5.9 | 6.4 | 4.0 | 7.5 | 5.7 | 4.8 | 2.6 | 2.0 | 2.1 |
| 5. Inflation adjusted structural balance | 6.5 | 5.1 | 2.7 | 0.6 | 5.4 | 5.3 | 0.7 | 3.6 | – 0.5 | 3.1 | 3.2 | 5.8 | 5.2 | 3.7 | 2.6 |
| 6. Alternative adjustment | 2.3 | 2.0 | 2.0 | 2.2 | 3.1 | 2.9 | 3.1 | 3.1 | 3.0 | 3.2 | 3.6 | 3.8 | 3.5 | 3.5 | 3.3 |
| 7. 'True' structural balance | 3.6 | 1.6 | – 0.1 | – 2.6 | – 2.6 | – 3.0 | – 2.1 | 0.3 | – 1.5 | – 1.2 | 1.1 | 4.8 | 6.1 | 3.8 | 3.8 |
| *Memo items* (£ billion, except*) | | | | | | | | | | | | | | | |
| Public sector financial deficit | – 0.7 | 0.3 | 1.6 | 2.8 | 4.8 | 7.6 | 8.5 | 6.1 | 8.3 | 8.6 | 11.2 | 9.1 | 7.7 | 10.8 | (13.9) |
| Bank of England inflation adjustments | 2.7 | 3.2 | 3.1 | 4.0 | 9.3 | 11.9 | 7.5 | 9.4 | 6.7 | 14.9 | 13.1 | 12.3 | 7.3 | 5.9 | (6.7) |

**Table 5.2** *continued*

| | 1970 | 1971 | 1972 | 1973 | 1974 | 1975 | 1976 | 1977 | 1978 | 1979 | 1980 | 1981 | 1982 | 1983 | 1984 |
|---|---|---|---|---|---|---|---|---|---|---|---|---|---|---|---|
| Public sector net monetary liabilities | 34.1 | 33.7 | 35.5 | 36.1 | 35.7 | 43.7 | 55.1 | 65.7 | 69.3 | 80.1 | 85.6 | 92.9 | 99.4 | 110.5 | 120.2 |
| Public sector net interest | 1.8 | 1.8 | 2.0 | 2.3 | 3.2 | 3.8 | 4.9 | 5.8 | 6.3 | 7.8 | 9.8 | 11.5 | 12.0 | 11.9 | (13.5) |
| GDP (expenditure) | 51.5 | 57.8 | 64.0 | 74.0 | 84.1 | 106.2 | 126.8 | 145.9 | 170.0 | 197.4 | 229.8 | 254.8 | 278.1 | 302.5 | 320.5 |
| Notes and coins | 3.8 | 4.1 | 4.3 | 4.8 | 5.4 | 6.2 | 6.9 | 7.6 | 8.8 | 9.9 | 10.7 | 11.3 | 11.6 | 12.1 | (12.7) |
| Inflation (%)* | 7.2 | 8.0 | 7.7 | 9.7 | 20.2 | 23.4 | 14.3 | 12.5 | 8.3 | 16.8 | 13.2 | 10.8 | 6.6 | 4.5 | 5.3 |

*Methods* ( + indicates surplus, − indicates deficit)
(Parentheses indicate estimates)
Line 1: % ratio of memo items 1 and 5 with sign changes
Line 2: from Price and Muller
Line 3: Sum of line 1 and line 2
Line 4: % ratio of memo items 2 and 5
Line 5: sum of line 3 and line 4
Line 6: (interest − $r_L$ = (NML − 2 (notes and coin))

$$\text{GDP}$$

where $r_L$ = 0.025 from 1970 to 1981 and 0.029 from 1982 and other items are as shown in memoranda
Line 7: sum of line 3 and line 6

*Sources*
Memo item 1: CSO *Economic Trends* (1984 estimates from FSBR 1985)
Memo item 2: *Bank of England Quarterly Bulletin*
Memo item 3: Public Sector Net Monetary Liabilities at Market Value (Bank of England)
Memo item 4: CSO NIE (1984 estimated from Public Expenditure White Paper)
Memo item 5: CSO Data Tape. GDP (expenditure) at market prices
Memo item 6: Miller and Babbs (1984) updated for 1983, 1984 using memo item 7
Memo item 7: *Bank of England Quarterly Bulletin*, CED deflator Qiv/Qiv

**Table 5.3**  Interest, inflation and public sector debt, 1970–84

| | 1970 | 1971 | 1972 | 1973 | 1974 | 1975 | 1976 | 1977 | 1978 | 1979 | 1980 | 1981 | 1982 | 1983 | 1984 |
|---|---|---|---|---|---|---|---|---|---|---|---|---|---|---|---|
| 1. Bank of England inflation adjustment/GDP | 5.2 | 5.5 | 4.8 | 5.4 | 11.1 | 11.2 | 5.9 | 6.4 | 4.0 | 7.5 | 5.7 | 4.8 | 2.6 | 2.0 | 2.1 |
| 2. Debt interest/GDP | 3.5 | 3.1 | 3.1 | 3.1 | 3.8 | 3.6 | 3.9 | 4.0 | 3.8 | 4.0 | 4.3 | 4.5 | 4.3 | 3.9 | 4.2 |
| 3. Treasury bill rate | 7.1 | 5.6 | 5.7 | 9.8 | 11.7 | 10.4 | 11.5 | 7.7 | 8.8 | 13.6 | 15.6 | 13.5 | 11.7 | 9.8 | 9.5 |
| 4. Inflation rate | 7.2 | 8.0 | 7.7 | 9.7 | 20.2 | 23.4 | 14.3 | 12.5 | 8.3 | 16.8 | 13.2 | 10.8 | 6.6 | 4.5 | 5.3 |
| 5. Nml/GDP, at nv | 73.8 | 67.6 | 63.7 | 57.4 | 54.3 | 49.8 | 50.3 | 49.7 | 46.6 | 44.7 | 41.5 | 41.7 | 39.2 | 37.7 | 38.5 |
| 6. Nml/GDP, at mv | 66.2 | 58.3 | 55.4 | 48.8 | 42.5 | 41.1 | 43.5 | 45.0 | 41.3 | 40.6 | 37.2 | 36.5 | 35.7 | 36.5 | 37.5 |
| 7. 'True cost'/GDP | 1.3 | 1.1 | 1.1 | 0.9 | 0.7 | 0.7 | 0.8 | 0.9 | 0.8 | 0.8 | 0.7 | 0.7 | 0.8 | 0.8 | 0.9 |

*Notes*
Line 1: see table 5.2, line 4
Line 2: see table 5.2, memo items
Line 3: Treasury bill yield, annual average, *Financial Statistics*
Line 5: Nominal value of net monetary liabilities deflated by GDP
Line 6: Market value of net monetary liabilities deflated by GDP
*Source of tables 5.2 and 5.3*
M. Miller, 'Measuring the stance of fiscal policy', *Oxford Review of Economic Policy*, 1/1 (Spring 1985)

line 3 of table 5.2 shows, after such correction the public sector financial balance was in substantial deficit throughout the 1970s and in substantial surplus in most of the 1980s. There can be little doubt that fiscal policy in itself did exert a contractionary influence on the economy in these years. Even so, it is noteworthy that the economy began to show major recovery in the years 1981–2 when the cyclically adjusted surplus was at its largest, suggesting that other factors affecting the private sector were becoming more important. Key among these was the decline in the real exchange rate, but the likely impact of the tight budget of 1981 on inflationary expectations and on confidence generally should not be ignored.

Quite apart from the practical difficulties inherent in cyclically adjusting the nominal budget deficit or surplus (in particular the problem of guessing potential output and incomes) other factors have to be considered. For instance, even if actual deficits are really surpluses after appropriate adjustment, deficits still have to be financed either through money creation or through sales of debt to the private sector. Also, adjusting the fiscal position for inflation could seem inappropriate at a time when the prime object of policy is to reduce inflation. At the very least we have to ask whether running the much larger actual budget deficits that would be implied by aiming at smaller adjusted surpluses would have created financing difficulties and added to inflationary pressures in the system.

The idea that if the Thatcher government had been prepared to run larger budget deficits it would have run into financing difficulties has been rejected on grounds that the ratio of public sector debt to GDP in the UK has fallen substantially in the post-war period and is now much lower than in many other OECD countries. The decline in the ratio was particularly fast in the decade of the 1970s, from over 0.68 in 1969 to 0.41 in 1979, falling to about 0.38 in 1984 (see table 5.3, line 6). Once again it has to be borne in mind that this apparent improvement in the public sector's financial position did not occur because of government success in containing actual deficits and borrowing: on the contrary, unadjusted public sector deficits averaged close to 5 per cent of GDP throughout these years (even though on a cyclical and inflation-adjusted basis budgets were in surplus rather than deficit!). Instead governments benefitted from high, and for most of the period, unanticipated inflation, which imposed a substantial inflation tax on debt holders, and from real interest rates which were generally below the rate of growth of real income and in most years even negative.

Although, on the face of it, the relatively low ratio of public sector debt in the UK in the 1980s does not suggest that the government would have been faced with a financing problem if it had run larger budget deficits – even though real interest rates have tended to be higher than real income growth – it would be a brave critic of the Thatcher strategy to put too much weight on this, given what happened in the decade of the 1970s. Presumably such critics would have argued in the 1970s – during which period unemployment was also rising and output growth slow – that fiscal policy should have aimed at even larger budget deficits than was then the case, even though national expenditure in nominal money terms was increasing at an annual average rate of over 15 per cent whilst inflation averaged over 12 per cent. If they were not prepared to argue this, the force of their criticism of fiscal policy in recent years would be greatly weakened. Perhaps it is just as well that governments in the 1970s were not aware that budgetary policy was so deflationary; otherwise they might have been tempted to run even larger unadjusted budget deficits!

They key, of course, is the relation between budget deficits and inflation: are the former the prime cause of the latter? It would be difficult to argue that budget deficits, either through their direct impact on the demand for goods and services or through an indirect effect via money creation, are or have been the prime cause of inflation. Nonetheless, it would be stretching a point to argue that deficits have no effect on inflation and that fiscal policy should ignore the inflationary pressures which are created elsewhere in the economy, even though in terms of output and employment the economy may be in recession.

While it can be reasonably argued that there were no 'solvency' or sound-finance grounds for the Thatcher policy of containing and reducing budget deficits in the years of the MTFS, it by no means follows that there were no grounds at all. In the last resort, the question whether or not fiscal and monetary policies were too tight throughout the years 1979–86 must be judged, from the demand management point of view, on their impact on the growth of *nominal* expenditure on goods and services. As far as the *balance* between fiscal and monetary policies is concerned (was the former too tight and the latter too loose, or vice versa?) the test would be the priority to be given to public or private sectors.

In the period 1979–86 nominal expenditure on goods and services increased at an annual average rate of about 9.5 per cent, falling from over 13 per cent per annum in the early years to less than 7 per cent at the end. If the object of the policy was to reduce inflation, the constraint on nominal expenditure growth does not seem excessive. Those critics advocating faster growth of nominal expenditure on grounds that output would have been higher, and would have increased at a faster rate, have to show that no supply constraint on output and employment existed and that faster inflation would not have absorbed most or all of the difference. If the 1970s are anything to go by, faster growth of nominal demand does not guarantee faster growth of real demand and real output, even when unemployment exists. Looser fiscal policy and tighter monetary policy might well have produced more employment, particularly if the looser fiscal policy had taken the form of higher public sector expenditure rather than lower taxation; but the manufacturing sector and the balance of payments might well have fared worse, owing to a stronger exchange rate.

It would be idle to pretend that considerations of 'sound' finance *per se* necessitated a radical change in fiscal policy in the 1980s. Nor can it be argued that unless fiscal policy were kept tight, it would be impossible to pursue anti-inflationary monetary policy. For reasons given earlier, a more correct view would seem to be that because the operation of monetary policy through monetary targeting involves unacceptably high costs in terms of interest rates and the exchange rate, imposing a severe burden on the private sector, more weight must be placed on fiscal policy for controlling inflation. But the MTFS can be defended on two grounds: first the linking together of fiscal and monetary policy was necessary if 'credibility' was to be restored to the government's anti-inflationary policy; and second, that by signalling the end of demand management, the government was looking for improved supply side performance. The justification for this will be discussed in chapter 7.

However, as a result of macroeconomic policy and other factors the problem of unemployment has become acute; and an important question is whether policy could have achieved better output and employment performance with no more inflation if the government had been willing to intervene more in wage determination. With this in mind, the next chapter will examine the nature and causes of unemployment in the British economy, with a view to assessing how far the government can be criticized for not dealing with it more efficiently even in the context of its own anti-inflationary strategy.

# 6

# The Strategy Criticized (2): Employment Policy

Unemployment is the difference between the supply of labour and the demand for it; thus unemployment will rise if the supply of labour rises faster than the demand for it or if demand falls relatively to supply. The increase in the supply of labour is determined by the growth of the population of working age (16 to 60 or 64 years) but also by the proportion of that working population which makes itself available for employment (the so-called 'activity' rate.) However, it seems clear that the activity rate is not independent of the demand for labour; the more work there is available, the greater is the number of people who look for it, and vice versa (for example, people may seek later or earlier retirement and married women may be more or less encouraged to seek work) so that to some extent the supply of labour is ambiguous.

In the UK, unemployment began to rise after the mid 1960s and had increased by more than 2.5 million people by 1984. During this period, population of working age increased by some 1.8 million, although the activity rate fell, producing an increase in the (available for) working population of around 1.4 million. Employment however declined by more than 1.3 million (including self-employment and the armed forces). Thus in purely arithmetical terms, half of the increase in unemployment was due to an increase in supply, and half due to a fall in demand.

The increase in the population of working age was particularly large in the period 1977–84, providing almost two-thirds of the total increase from the mid 1960s. Thus, in effect, the economy had to run faster after 1977 than in the decade before simply to stay where it was in terms of unemployment. In fact, it did not: employment fell by more than 1.2

**Table 6.1** Unemployment, new basis (UK claimants excluding school-leavers)

|  | Total (000s) | Male (%) | Female (%) | Total (%) |
|---|---|---|---|---|
| 1975 | 860.6 | 4.3 | 1.7 | 3.3 |
| 1976 | 1,178.5 | 5.6 | 2.7 | 4.5 |
| 1977 | 1,250.6 | 5.8 | 3.1 | 4.8 |
| 1978 | 1,226.0 | 5.5 | 3.3 | 4.7 |
| 1979 | 1,140.5 | 5.0 | 3.1 | 4.3 |
| 1980 | 1,451.7 | 6.3 | 4.0 | 5.4 |
| 1981 | 2,269.8 | 10.1 | 5.9 | 8.5 |
| 1982 | 2,626.1 | 11.7 | 6.9 | 9.9 |
| 1983 | 2,865.9 | 12.7 | 7.7 | 10.7 |
| 1984 | 2,998.3 | 12.9 | 8.3 | 11.1 |
| 1985 | 3,113.1 | 13.1 | 8.6 | 11.3 |
| 1986 (Oct.) | 3,194.0 | 13.3 | 8.9 | 11.6 |
| 1987 (Sept.) | 2,775.3 |  |  | 10.0 |

*Source*: National Economic Development Office, *The British Labour Market and Unemployment*, (NEDC, Feb. 1987), 16, annexe 2

million, and unemployment rose by more than 1.7 million despite a sharp decline (equivalent to almost half a million people) in the activity rate. While, no doubt, the UK economy would have had difficulty in the best of times to absorb such a large increase in the supply of labour available to it without a decline in the activity rate, the decline in demand for labour made things much worse, leaving government policy open to severe criticism.

As table 6.1 shows, unemployment rose rapidly in the early years of the 1980s, more than doubling between 1979 and 1982. Thereafter, it rose more slowly, appearing to stabilize through 1985–6, before falling through 1986–7. We may begin therefore by posing two questions: how far was the government responsible for the massive rise through 1979–83, and could it have done more to pull unemployment down again after 1983?

As far as the first question is concerned, it has to be recognized at the outset that unemployment was no new problem for the UK, even in the post-war period: it had risen sharply through the 1970s, more than doubling between 1970 and 1979. Moreover, the 1979–80 oil price rise (oil price more than doubled in these years) triggered off world recession from which the UK could not remain immune. The attempt to put all

**Table 6.2**   Unemployment rates

|             | 1979 | 1986 |
|-------------|------|------|
| US          | 5.8  | 7.0  |
| Japan       | 2.1  | 2.7  |
| Germany     | 3.2  | 8.0  |
| France      | 5.9  | 10.2 |
| UK          | 5.1  | 12.0 |
| Italy       | 7.6  | 11.0 |
| Belgium     | 8.2  | 13.0 |
| Denmark     |      | 8.5  |
| Ireland     |      | 17.2 |
| Netherlands |      | 14.0 |
| Spain       |      | 21.7 |

*Source*: (OECD), *Economic Outlook* 39 (May 1986)

the blame on the Thatcher administration overlooks the fact that most
other industrial countries also suffered from rising unemployment in
the 1980s, some worse than the UK (see table 6.2), although it is true
that the UK went into recession earlier than most.[1] Nor should it be
forgotten that the UK's newly assumed oil producer status, which
coincided with the massive rise in the world price of oil, was bound to
have an adverse impact on UK manufacturing for reasons discussed
earlier. Nonetheless, the severity of the downturn in the UK had much
to do with the sharp tightening of monetary policy in the UK which
pushed up interest rates and the exchange rate, thereby exacerbating
the impact of these factors (North Sea oil, oil price rise and world
recession) on UK manufacturing. Although the attempt to pull down
inflation from the high levels of the 1970s was bound to be associated
with some rise in unemployment, the government undoubtedly underestimated the tightness of the monetary policy it was pursuing in 1979–
80 (for reasons we have discussed in the previous chapter),[2] and also
overestimated the flexibility of the labour market and of real wages in
response to growing unemployment.

Monetary policy was soon relaxed, and interest rates and the
exchange rate fell. Output recovered after 1981 and continued to expand

1 The UK went into recession in the second half of 1979; other major
OECD countries followed nine to twelve months later.
2 See ch. 5, pp. 98–104.

at a reasonable rate in the following years. Yet unemployment continued to rise, although at a much less rapid rate, before peaking out in 1986 at a level well in excess of 3 million. Thus, despite significant output recovery after 1981 the UK seems to have been left with a chronic unemployment problem, unresponsive to output growth.

The government's general approach to unemployment was to emphasize the excessive level of the real wage and the cost of labour which priced labour out of work, rather than Keynesian aggregate demand deficiency; and, in the first term of its period in office, to look for the solution in the normal working of the labour market (excess supply of labour should push down the real wage, pricing people back into work). In what follows therefore we shall examine the real wage – unemployment argument, and then consider how it is that the labour market failed to bring about a level of wages at which full employment, or at any rate a much higher level of employment, could be restored.

## Real Wages and Unemployment

The view that unemployment is in the last resort due to the *real* wage being too high has a respectable lineage, and, as has been pointed out in chapter 1, was by no means rejected by Keynes himself. Of course, hardly any economist would deny that, in a profit-seeking private enterprise economy, the real wage and the demand for labour are related, although there would be disagreement about the effectiveness of labour markets for bringing about the real wage at which everybody seeking work can get it. In theoretical terms, the real wage can be too high for the achievement and maintenance of full employment – too high in the *short run sense* that, given the stock of capital and state of technology, the real wage being demanded by the suppliers of labour is greater than the marginal or marginal revenue product of labour *at full employment level of output* (not, be it noted, higher than the marginal revenue product of labour at the *existing* level of output and employment – see later), and in the *long run sense* that, given the rate of technological progress and application, it encourages the substitution of capital for labour at a faster rate than would otherwise have occurred, and faster than is consistent with absorbing the natural increase in the labour supply.

Many economists, even those who fully accept that real wage pressure has been an important contributory factor to the rise in unemployment in the UK in the last decade or so, find difficulty in discussing the problem in these terms. The reason is that in practice workers and employers negotiate in terms of nominal money wages, not real wages. Real wages emerge as a result of actual money wage and price behaviour, and therefore appear endogenous to the system rather than exogenous. Moreover, even if we take the stock of capital and the state of technology as given, a unique relationship between employment and the real wage need not necessarily be expected. Entrepreneurs typically price their products by adding a profit mark-up to their direct costs (i.e. labour plus material costs). This profit mark-up is naturally a function of the state or degree of competition, but it is also affected by the level of demand for the entrepreneurs' products. When this demand is high, an entrepreneur can take advantage by increasing his profit mark-up; and he may or may not increase employment. This, temporarily at least, tends to alter the relationship between the product price and the money wage (i.e. the real product wage) whether or not employment is affected. In case of a decline in demand for product, for example, the entrepreneur may respond by reducing his profit mark-up rather than by reducing output and employment. Thus the own product real wage may rise, although employment does not fall.[3]

While this is true, it is by no means the whole story; the analysis has to be extended further. Although the worker may bargain in terms of money wages, he undoubtedly has real wage objectives in mind. An entrepreneur who, because of the demand situation has been able to raise his profit mark-up, i.e. lower the product real wage, may find that as a consequence he has to pay higher money wages in the next pay round. Given the state of demand for his product, he may have to lower his profit margin, perhaps back to its previous level, or reduce employment. The previous relationship between product price, money wage and employment may be restored. Similarly, a temporary willingness to accept lower profit margins in order to maintain output and employment in the face of a decline in demand for a product may not be extended to a willingness to accept a permanently lower return on capital or lower reward to entrepreneurship. Output may be cut back or an attempt made to raise labour productivity through improved labour working practices or substitution of capital for labour, so that employment eventually falls.

3 That the relationship between the real wage and the level of employment could change in the short run owing to a change in the 'degree of monopoly', i.e. a change in the ratio of price to marginal revenue, was pointed out by M. Kalecki soon after the *General Theory* appeared. See M. Kalecki, 'The determinants of the distribution of income', *Econometrica*, April 1938.

We can apply this analysis to a situation where trade union militancy or external economic shock such as a massive oil price rise impact on the product and labour markets, as happened in the UK in the 1970s. For example, suppose there is an autonomous and permanent rise in trade union militancy which, in a given market context, puts substantial upward and widespread pressure on money wages: labour costs therefore rise. Given aggregate demand for goods and services in nominal money terms, prices may not be initially raised. Output is therefore not affected, so that labour has achieved a rise in the product real wage without a fall in employment. The process could presumably end there if entrepreneurs are willing permanently to accept a cut in their profit margins (i.e. a fall in the degree of monopoly); but while some permanent decline in profit margins (i.e. a rise in the share of labour in value added) might be conceivable, there is clearly a limit to the long run ability of militant trade unions to raise product real wages and income share at the expense of the entrepreneurs. Sooner or later, prices will be raised, so moving the product real wage back towards its initial level.[4]

In a limiting case, profit margins are fully restored, and profit margins are back where they started. However, given the level of *nominal* demand, output and employment are lower and prices are higher. There is then a temptation to argue that, because the product real wage is not higher, higher unemployment cannot be due to higher real wages; but the *non sequitur* is obvious. It is the *attempt* to get a higher product real wage at the *same level of employment* which underlies the fall in employment. In classical language the desired product real wage is above the marginal revenue product of labour at the existing level of employment: hence the level of employment cannot be sustained. Indeed, it is the failure to recognize that it is the *desired* real wage at full employment relative to the marginal or marginal revenue product of labour at full employment – and not the *existing* real wage – which is important that vitiates a number of studies which purport to show that the real wage is not excessive.

Governments could (and British governments prior to Thatcher have typically done so!) validate the higher price level by taking policy measures to increase nominal demand for goods and services – in other words, to acquiesce in inflation. As a result, when prices rise,

---

4 A long-lasting reduction in the profit mark-up will tend to reduce the real rate of return on capital, and therefore eventually reduce the supply of capital and the level of investment. The incautious economist then blames the resulting fall in employment on insufficient investment – a Keynesian explanation!

output and employment are not affected. Equally, however, trade unions will not have succeeded, except perhaps temporarily during the time-lag between costs rising and prices rising, in obtaining higher product real wages; so they may try again. At some point the government will have to constrain the inflation by constraining nominal demand. A fall in output and employment then eventually ensues, although unions may have succeeded at least partly in achieving the rise in the real wage. The unions (supported even by some economists) then blame the government for restrictive macroeconomic policy rather than themselves for the consequential unemployment.

It is evident that 'too high a real wage' cannot be dismissed as a cause of rising unemployment simply because actual real wages have not risen in the process, although it might be better to state the cause more precisely, as upward pressure on the real wage.

The dismissal of 'too high a real wage' as being the cause of unemployment when real wages have in fact not risen may also be misleading in the case of external shocks to the economy. A permanent or at any rate long-lasting rise in the real price of imported inputs to the economy (i.e. a rise in the nominal prices of those inputs relatively to the nominal price of final output) will tend to reduce the *ex ante* demand for labour and raise the price level. (The demand for labour falls because the rise in input prices to the economy directly lowers the marginal revenue product of labour – measured net of the cost of the inputs – at all levels of employment). Thus product real wages must now fall if employment is to be maintained. If money wage demands respond in the upward direction to the rise in the price and not in the downward direction to the reduction in demand for labour, inflation and unemployment will result. As before, if government steps in to stop inflation without there having been a willingness on the part of the labour force to accept a cut in the product real wage (assuming unchanged labour productivity) in response to the country's (or industry's) worsening terms of trade, unemployment will settle at a higher level. The attempt to accommodate the rise in the price level by pumping in demand in nominal money terms will accelerate the inflation triggered off by rising import prices, whilst only temporarily at best staving off the inevitable rise in unemployment.

Debate on the question whether the rise in unemployment in the UK, and in other industrial countries as well, in the 1970s and 1980s was due to demand deficiency or 'too high real wages' has been intense and a less than full consensus has been achieved. Credence is given to the view that 'too high a real wage' is the main, or at any rate an important cause, by very dissimilar developments in the US and Europe. In the US, real earnings fell by 13 per cent in the decade 1972–82 whilst total employment rose by over 20 per cent. Although rising sharply in the immediate post first oil price shock – induced recession, unemployment fell equally sharply in the following years (from 8.5 per cent of the labour force in 1975 to around 7 per cent in 1980). Policy tightening after the second oil price shock of 1979–80 led to a rise in unemployment through 1980–2, but by 1985 unemployment was back to less than 8 per cent of the labour force. Even though real hourly earnings began to rise again in 1982, they were barely back to their 1970 level by 1985, whilst employment continued to rise.

In Europe, the picture was very different. Real hourly earnings continued to rise in all of the main European countries after the first oil price shock, and despite some slackening off in the early years of the 1980s they remained significantly above the level of the early 1970s. In the UK real wages were 18 per cent higher whilst employment was 10 per cent lower. Of course, the productivity of labour also enters into the relationship between product real wages and employment; and we should note that in the latter years of our period 'whole economy' productivity grew a good deal less rapidly in the US than in European countries, a fact which clearly contributed to the US's better employment performance.[5] However, as has been argued earlier, the behaviour of productivity is not independent of the real wage since the cost of labour clearly affects the decision to substitute capital for labour, and it seems likely that the greater willingness of the US labour force to accept restraint on real wage behaviour than was the case in Europe meant that the pressure to substitute capital for labour (which would have raised productivity) was a good deal less in the US than in Europe.

Research into the relative contribution of demand deficiency and excessive real wages to high and rising unemployment is not easy, and results are seldom conclusive. Most of the major research in this area is too voluminous to be described and can only be summarized here.[6] It suggests, not surprisingly, that the behaviour of real wages has had an important influence on employment, particularly in the last decade

5 In the 1980s, 'whole economy' productivity in the four major European countries rose by about 2.25% per annum compared with 1.4% in the US. Employment in the European countries rose by less than 0.25% per annum compared with almost 2.5% per annum in the US see OECD, *Economic Outlook*).

6 See G.D.N. Worswick and R. Gansden, 'Real wages and employment', NIESR Discussion Paper no. 122, for a very useful review of some of the evidence. For a revealing comparison of the relationship between the real wage and employment in the UK and the US, see also 'Employment creation in the US and the UK', *Bank of England Quarterly Bulletin* Vol. 26, No. 3 (Sept. 1986).

and a half. Although approaches to the problem have differed, there seems general agreement on a number of points, viz.: (i) a wage explosion in Europe in the 1970s, which was partly due to trade union militancy and partly triggered by the steep rise in imported material prices, particularly energy, was a major factor underlying the *growth* of unemployment;[7] (ii) the US and Japan suffered less from wage explosion in this period than did Europe, partly because money wages responded less (in an upward direction) to the rise in import prices than (in the downward direction) to the rise in unemployment;[8] (iii) the wage explosion in the 1970s was worse in the UK than in most other countries, and with the rise in energy prices accounted for the UK's worse employment experience;[9] (iv) demand deficiency was possibly a more important factor in the 1980s than it was in the 1970s, even in the UK – although it could be that the surge in unemployment witnessed in Europe in 1980–2 was due to the length of the time-lag for rising real wages to feed into unemployment;[10] and (v) even if demand deficiency was more important in Europe in the 1980s than in the 1970s, it is still the case that the share of labour in final output was well in excess of that warranted in a high employment situation, and that real wages are still incompatible with a high level of employment in manufacturing, a conclusion which applies with particular force to the UK.[11]

In an analysis of the impact of the 1973 terms of trade (oil price) shock on the economies of the industrial developed world, Professor Bruno and Professor Sachs have attempted to identify the labour market and other characteristics which seemed to determine how badly countries were affected in terms of unemployment and inflation.[12]

7 See, for example: J. Symons and R. Layard, 'Neo-classical demand for labour functions for 6 major economies', *Economic Journal*, 94/376 (Dec. 1984), pp. 788–99 and A. Newell and J.S.V. Symons, 'Wages and employment in the OECD countries', Centre for Labour Economics, LSE, Discussion Paper (May 1985), no. 219.

8 Newell and Symons, 'Wages and Employment'.

9 P.R.G. Layard, and S.J. Nickell, 'Unemployment, real wages and aggregate demand in Europe, Japan, and the US', Centre for Labour Economics, LSE, Discussion Paper (Mar. 1985), no. 214.

10 Layard and Nickell, 'Unemployment, real wages and aggregate demand' also G. Basevi, O. Blanchard, W. Bucler, R. Dornbusch and R. Layard, 'Macroeconomic prospects and policies for the European Community', Centre for European Policy Studies, Internal Paper (Apr. 1983), no. 12.

11 J.R. Artus, 'The disequilibrium real wage hypothesis: an empirical evaluation', *IMF Staff Papers*, 31 2 (June 1984).

12 M. Bruno and G. Sachs, *The Economics of Worldwide Stagflation* (Blackwell, Oxford, 1985).

They show that those countries that were affected worse were characterized, first, by having a rather 'decentralized' wage bargaining
system and, second, by having strong trade unions able to push up
money wages in line with prices. Countries such as Norway, Sweden
and Austria with centralized wage bargaining institutions through
which the state imposes an effective, almost permanent incomes
policy, escaped relatively lightly since appropriate wage adjustments
could be more easily made to the oil price shock. The UK, on the other
hand, with its rather decentralized bargaining system and its strong,
politically supported trade unions, came off badly, despite attempts by
the government of the day to get agreement on wages and incomes.
Typically, both pre and post oil price shock, money wages have been
highly responsive to price increases and very insensitive to the labour
demand and unemployment. The insensitivity of the real wage to external shocks and rising unemployment, coupled with a macroeconomic
policy that generally accommodated inflationary pressures, con-
demned the UK to rapid inflation, without however avoiding the
increase in unemployment that was inevitable.

Thus the Thatcher government's insistence that unemployment in
the UK is related to the real wage cannot easily be dismissed; nor can its
reluctance to resort to Keynesian demand expansion as a means of
reducing it be criticized, given the failure of that kind of policy in the
1970s. But if determination not to accommodate inflationary pressures
has been successful in pulling down inflation, rising unemployment
does not seem to have increased the flexibility of the real wage. The
labour market has refused to behave in the classical way, despite
increasing government efforts to make it do so.

### Inefficient Labour Market

That this is so is brought out clearly in table 6.3. Wage inflation slowed
down sharply from 1979 to 1982 but then appears to have stabilized at
around 8 per cent, despite unemployment exceeding 3 million (around
11 per cent of the labour force). At the same time consumption real
wages have risen steadily, showing no signs of being affected by rising
unemployment.

Indeed the elasticity of the real wage with respect to unemployment –
that is, the proportional change in the real wage in response to a given
change in the rate of unemployment (not to be confused with the proportional change in the demand for labour in response to a given change
in the real wage) – appears very low. Table 6.4 summarizes the findings

**Table 6.3**   Annual growth of earnings and retail price inflation

|  | *Average weekly earnings (%)* | *Retail price index (%)* | *Unemployment (% labour force)* |
|---|---|---|---|
| 1975 | 23.6 | 21.7 | 3.3 |
| 1976 | 14.3 | 15.3 | 4.5 |
| 1977 | 9.8 | 14.7 | 4.8 |
| 1978 | 13.4 | 7.9 | 4.7 |
| 1979 | 14.5 | 12.6 | 4.3 |
| 1980 | 17.2 | 16.5 | 5.4 |
| 1981 | 12.1 | 11.2 | 8.5 |
| 1982 | 8.9 | 8.3 | 9.9 |
| 1983 | 8.1 | 4.5 | 10.7 |
| 1984 | 5.9 | 4.9 | 11.1 |
| 1985 | 8.1 | 5.9 | 11.3 |
| 1986 (Sept.) | 7.9 | 3.4 | 10.4 |

*Source*: National Economic Development Office, *The British Labour Market and Unemployment*, (NEDC, 1987), annexe 8

**Table 6.4**   Elasticities of the real wage with respect to unemployment, UK

| *Author* | *Elasticity* | *Sector* |
|---|---|---|
| Carruth and Oswald (1986) | – 0.05 | Non-manufacturing |
|  | – 0.04 | Manufacturing |
| Hall and Henry (1987) | – 0.08[a] | Economy |
| Layard and Nickell (1985) | – 0.07 | Economy |
| Newell and Symons (1986) | – 0.06 | Manufacturing |
| Nickell (1986) | – 0.09 | Economy |
| Smith and Holly (1985) | – 0.08 | Non-manufacturing |
|  | – 0.16 | Manufacturing |

[a] For Hall and Henry (1987) the elasticity is estimated from a linear unemployment variable at 10% unemployment.
*Source*: National Economic Development Office, *The British Labour Market and Unemployment* (NEDC, 1987), 16, annexe

of a number of studies, from which it will be seen that elasticities of less than – 0.1 are common. The implication is that a massive rise in unemployment appears to be required to achieve a significant fall in the real wage. Moreover, the elasticity seems to decline as unemployment increases: i.e. real wages become less responsive to unemployment, the more unemployment there is.[13]

Table 6.3 indicates that inflation was falling when unemployment was rising, but it also indicates that inflation stopped declining around 1983/4 once unemployment reached 11 per cent. Part of the explanation of this apparently ominous development could lie in faster productivity growth in industry, particularly manufacturing, referred to earlier. This has allowed industry to pay substantial money wage increases to its labour force without pushing up labour costs per unit of output. However, money wages in non-manufacturing sectors of the economy, particularly services, where productivity rises much less fast, have kept pace. Service prices have therefore risen, resulting in general inflation. Such a development, often referred to as 'productivity-gap' inflation[14] can take place without undermining the country's international trading competitiveness.

Even so, there is a suggestion that the non-accelerating rate of inflation level of unemployment (the NAIRU, referred to in chapter 2) has risen substantially during the Thatcher period. If that is so, it would mean that a further decline in the rate of inflation – which is the government's long term aim – would require a further rise in unemployment; alternatively, that expanding aggregate demand to increase employment will sooner or later lead to an increase in inflation. But why should the NAIRU have risen in this way?

One explanation would be an increase in the bargaining power of worker organizations, including the trade unions. But the government has made determined efforts to cut back the power of trade unions, partly through the legislation described in chapter 4, partly through its support of management in struggles to improve work practices and productivity (for example, the Wapping dispute between the print workers and News International), and partly through a willingness to stand up to long and bitter strikes, such as that entered into by the coal miners in 1984. None of the usual indicators suggests that trade union power over wage settlements has increased in recent years; if anything, the evidence goes the other way (see table 6.5). The general consensus is

13   A. Carruth and A. Oswald, 'Wage inflexibility in Britain', Centre for Labour Economics, LSE Discussion Paper 1986 no. 258.

14   For a discussion of 'productivity-gap' inflation, see G. Maynard and W. van Ryckeghem, *A World of Inflation* (Batsford, London, 1976), pp. 17–20.

**Table 6.5**  Indicators of union influence

| | Union membership as % of employment | No. of stoppages | Days lost per 1,000 employees |
|---|---|---|---|
| 1977 | 58.0 | 2,737 | 408 |
| 1978 | 58.3 | 2,498 | 376 |
| 1979 | 58.6 | 2,125 | 1,162 |
| 1980 | 59.2 | 1,348 | 473 |
| 1981 | 57.4 | 1,344 | 175 |
| 1982 | 56.3 | 1,538 | 222 |
| 1983 | 54.4 | 1,364 | 158 |
| 1984 | 52.6 | 1,221 (miners' strike) | 1,133 |
| 1985 | 50.9 | 903 | 266 |

*Source*: National Economic Development Office, *The British Labour Market and Unemployment* (NEDC, 1987), 16, annexe 2

that the trade unions have had less power under the Thatcher government than under previous governments, Conservative or Labour.[15]

An alternative explanation would be increasing unwillingness of the labour force to accept existing real wage levels, quite apart from trade union power and influence: in effect, the labour supply has contracted in relation to existing demand, forcing a rise in the real wage at a higher level of unemployment. Labour might be induced to behave in this way if the attraction of state financed unemployment benefits was increased. Here again, the government has moved in the opposite direction by reducing unemployment benefits in relation to pay whilst at the same time cutting marginal rates of tax. The evidence marshalled in table 6.6 does not suggest that the labour force would have done significantly better in the 1980s than in the 1970s by staying out of employment, although there are a number of economists who would take a different view.[16] Changes in the administration of unemployment benefits may have made those benefits easier to obtain, thereby

15  It is politically significant that by 1987 there were more shareholders in British companies than there were trade unionists (9.2 million versus 9 million).

16  For a contrary view, see P. Minford, D. Davies, M. Peel and A. Sprague, *Unemployment: Cause and Cure* (Martin Robertson, Oxford, 1983).

**Table 6.6**   The ratio of unemployment benefits to average earnings net of tax

|  | Micklewright I | Mickle-wright II | Layard & Nickell | Sentance |
|---|---|---|---|---|
|  | *(incl. earnings related benefits)* *(%)* | *(%)* | *(incl. social and housing benefits)* *(%)* | *(%)* |
| 1970 | 68.7 | 46.1 | 51.2 | 42.2 |
| 1971 | 63.3 | 40.9 | 50.6 | 41.8 |
| 1972 | 66.7 | 43.8 | 47.0 | 40.1 |
| 1973 | 65.0 | 44.4 | 46.6 | 37.4 |
| 1974 | 65.2 | 43.4 | 47.2 | 37.5 |
| 1975 | 65.6 | 47.5 | 49.2 | 39.6 |
| 1976 | 64.7 | 45.9 | 50.0 | 41.0 |
| 1977 | 67.5 | 47.8 | 51.3 | 40.9 |
| 1978 | 64.2 | 46.4 | 49.8 | 39.8 |
| 1979 | 59.1 | 43.2 | 46.0 | 36.5 |
| 1980 | 55.9 | 41.7 | 45.8 | 38.4 |
| 1981 | 52.2 | 41.5 | 50.3 | 41.6 |
| 1982 | 40.7 | 40.7 | 53.5 | 42.8 |
| 1983 | 40.6 | 40.6 | 54.4 | 43.1 |
| 1984 | 40.0 | 40.0 |  | 41.3 |
| 1985 | 39.0 | 39.0 |  | 41.6 |
| 1986 | 38.3 | 38.3 |  |  |

*Source*: National Economic Development Office, *The British Labour Market and Unemployment* (NEDC, 1987), 16, annexe 2

bringing more people into the category of those preferring unemployment to employment, and a growing black market may have provided opportunities for untaxed work for people nominally unemployed and still collecting unemployment benefits; but there is little hard evidence to suggest that either of these has had a significant impact on the unemployment–real wage relationship.

Given the difficulty of interpreting that relationship in terms of classical supply side behaviour, alternative explanations have been sought, and a plausible one is based on a distinction between *insiders* and *outsiders* in the labour force. Insiders are those who have secure full-time jobs and are able to exert wage pressure. The interests of outsiders (those without secure full-time jobs although possibly with part-time ones) are ignored; and because these outsiders have no say in the bargaining process, real wages are pushed up so that they become gradually but permanently excluded from full-time employment. In theory, the outsiders should be able to displace the insiders by offering their labour at a lower price (thereby reducing the bargaining power of the insiders), but there are a number of factors hindering their ability to do this. For example, there are straightforward hiring, firing and training costs, which reduce the firm's willingness to replace existing workers by new workers even at a lower wage. Employers have little or no *ex ante* knowledge of the skills and diligence of outsiders and it may be costly to find out by hiring them or training them subsequently. Providing the insiders are doing their job reasonably satisfactorily, employers will not quickly look elsewhere. Moreover, pay negotiations take time and must in the first instance be conducted with insiders or their trade unions: outsiders do not have unions to negotiate for them. Unless there is a substantial turnover of firms – new ones seeking new labour – outsiders are progressively pushed into the ranks of the long term or permanently unemployed. Pockets of long term unemployment, often regionally located, are created, whose impact on the level of national pay settlements is virtually zero. In effect, these people are no longer part of the country's labour force and play no part in wage bargaining. Only those members of the labour force who have recently become unemployed (i.e. the short term unemployed) have an impact on pay settlements, so that the trade-off between inflation and unemployment applies to these people only and not to the long term unemployed. Short term unemployment would have to be increased to pull inflation down further. Thus, as the *proportion* of the long term unemployed in the total rises, the influence of unemployment on the real wage and on inflation declines. In the jargon of the economist, the NAIRU rises.

Support for this contention can be found by comparing table 6.6 with table 6.7. Between 1979 and 1986, the number of men who have been unemployed for more than 12 months rose by 759,000 while those unemployed for more than 24 months rose by 522,000. The proportion of total unemployment represented by those unemployed for more than a year rose from 29 per cent to nearly 55 per cent. Moreover, whilst the numbers of unemployed for less than a year peaked out in 1981, those unemployed for longer continued to rise strongly.

It is therefore evident that the labour market, left to itself, has failed to deal with the unemployment problem, and indeed the government was excessively optimistic to believe that it would. In fact, given the causes underlying the rise in unemployment since 1979, it was most unlikely that it could.

**Table 6.7**    Male unemployment in the United Kingdom

|      | *Less than 12 months* | *More than 12 months* | *More than 24 months* |
|------|-----------------------|-----------------------|-----------------------|
| 1975 | 667,000               | 132,000               |                       |
| 1976 | 790,000               | 194,000               |                       |
| 1977 | 781,000               | 252,000               |                       |
| 1978 | 744,000               | 268,000               |                       |
| 1979 | 659,000               | 269,000               | 143,000               |
| 1980 | 896,000               | 289,000               | 165,000               |
| 1981 | 1,444,000             | 467,000               | 223,000               |
| 1982 | 1,413,000             | 818,000               | 387,000               |
| 1983 | 1,339,000             | 903,000               | 463,000               |
| 1984 | 1,245,000             | 953,000               | 585,000               |
| 1985 | 1,239,000             | 1,020,000             | 654,000               |
| 1986 | 1,239,000             | 1,028,000             | 665,000               |

*Source*: National Economic Development Office, *The British Labour Market and Unemployment*, (NEDC, 1987), 16, annexe 2

## Structural and Regional Factors

The 1.3 million increase in the long term unemployed corresponds very broadly to the decline in employment in UK manufacturing industry (6.6 million in 1979 compared with 5.3 million in 1986). Thus, superficially at least, all can be blamed on the monetarist policies of 1979–81 which, by forcing up interest rates and the exchange rate, rendered much of British industry uncompetitive. But if 'monetarism' was the spark that fired the explosion of unemployment, the gunpowder had certainly been well and truly laid much earlier. There would be little disagreement that much of UK manufacturing industry in the 1970s was excessively overmanned and afflicted by low labour and capital productivity. Substantial amounts of labour were employed in declining industries, such as iron and steel and shipbuilding, which survived only because of massive government financial assistance. A huge shake-up of manufacturing industry, with a shake-out of labour, were sooner or later inevitable, and the longer it was delayed the more horrendous were the employment consequences likely to be. It was fortunate for the UK that the shake-out of labour which occurred in the 1980s, and the inevitable initial decline in manufacturing output that was bound to accompany it, coincided with North Sea oil coming

on stream at a high world price. Without the protection this provided for the UKs balance of payments and the standard of living, the social and economic costs of the overdelayed restructuring of British industry would have been much greater, and possibly insupportable in political terms.

It is clear that the very substantial rise in labour productivity that has taken place in manufacturing industry since 1979 could not have been obtained at unchanged levels of employment. By 1986 manufacturing productivity was up some 40 per cent as compared with 1979,[17] implying that manufacturing output would have to be greater by a similar amount if employment were to be maintained. Given the world recession of the early 1980s and the pressure on other non-oil producing industrial countries to increase their net exports of manufactures, it seems unlikely that the UK could have achieved the necessary increase in its own net exports of manufactures.

Although the greatly improved productivity performance of British industry augurs well for the future as North Sea oil runs out, it is very unlikely that manufacturing will provide a source of employment on the scale of the 1970s. In the longer run, that must be provided by the services sector of the economy, including the services provided by the government. However, employment in the *private* services sector of the economy is closely dependent on productivity and real wages in the manufacturing sector. On the one hand, low productivity, and therefore low real wages and incomes in manufacturing, restricts the demand for ancillary and personal services; on the other hand, the closer real wages in manufacturing are to the minimum acceptable standard of living, the less willing are those without jobs to accept cuts in wages to get employment in services. Thus although unemployment breeds poverty, poverty also breeds unemployment. Despite the substantial rise in productivity in UK manufacturing in recent years, the UK still remains a relatively low productivity and low real wage economy.[18] Private service employment is therefore inhibited. Employment in the government service sector (for example, the National Health Service), is less inhibited (although offered at low real wages) since the services are provided free of charge, or at nominal charge, to the consumer. Even so, as recent British experience shows, a reluctance of the taxpayer to pay ever higher taxes relatively to income

17 See P. Spencer, *Britain's Productivity Renaissance*, (Credit Suisse First Boston Securities, June 1987).

18 G.F. Ray, 'Labour Costs in Manufacturing', *National Institute Economic Review*, 120 May 1987.

imposes a limit on employment even in the government services sector.

Unfortunately lack of employment opportunities in services due to low productivity or falling employment in manufacturing has a regional dimension. The decline of manufacturing has been particularly great in the north of the country and has reduced opportunities for employment in services. Concentrations of high unemployment have been left in these regions, whilst most of the employment opportunities can be found elsewhere.

Government response to this problem, as well as to that created by 'outsiders', is to point to the need for labour mobility and for regional, rather than national, pay policies that would reflect excess supply of labour. In principle, labour mobility would reduce the supply of labour in areas of high unemployment whilst lower real wages in those areas would attract firms to set up there rather than in higher labour cost areas. As to the 'outsiders', a willingness on their part to accept the lower real wages that would offset turnover costs can be expected over time to reduce the disadvantage suffered by them, *vis à vis* the insiders, and would bring about greater overall real wage moderation and therefore increased demand for labour.

However, it is unrealistic to believe that labour mobility can play a significant role in reducing long term unemployment in the areas afflicted, very largely in the depressed northern half of the country. A big obstacle is the enormous discrepancy in rents and house prices between the north and the south, where job opportunities exist. The increase in pay that would be necessary to compensate a worker for moving south is unrealistically large and not on offer. Moreover, decades of rent control have precluded an ample supply of rental accommodation throughout the country, inhibiting labour mobility generally. Regional pay differentials, if substantial enough, should in principle lead to some re-siting of existing firms and the location of new ones. Unfortunately, many of the present areas of high long term unemployment have a long history of labour unrest, restrictive practices and frequent strikes which has to be overcome. Thus the reliance on the workings of the free market to bring about an appropriate relocation of jobs and workers that would solve the regional unemployment quickly seems excessively optimistic. Therefore critics of the government are probably right to press for different policies, particularly for those which focus directly on the unemployment problem. But what policies are they?

## Alternative Policies for Employment

As one would expect, those critics who see the problem solely in terms of deficient aggregate demand, press for larger budget deficits and easier monetary policy, i.e. for general demand reflation. Others, recognizing that inflation remains a potential problem, would support an increase in public sector employment financed by an increase in taxation (i.e. no increase in the budget deficit), or would link an expansion of aggregate demand with measures to restrain money wages and prices. Others put more emphasis on special measures aimed more directly at specific areas of unemployment.

Since the product real wage is not a restraint on employment in the public sector (in the same way as it is for the profit seeking private sector), it could be argued that the government should increase employment simply by increasing its own expenditure on particular public sector projects or services. Even if public sector measures to increase employment are directed at the long term unemployed – so mitigating upward pressure on money wages – other repercussions have to be taken into account. If the increase in public expenditure is financed by higher taxes, the existing work force may respond by demanding higher money wages to protect disposable real incomes and/or consumption real wages. The supply price of labour to the private sector then rises, tending to reduce employment there. The current account of the balance of payments may worsen, leading to exchange rate depreciation, thereby adding to inflationary pressures already existing in the economy. If the increase in public sector expenditure is financed by debt finance, i.e. issuing government bonds, the exchange rate could actually *appreciate*, thereby worsening the trade balance and reducing employment in the private sector. If financed by money creation, the increase in public sector expenditure may add to existing inflationary pressures. Thus, while not to be ruled out, measures to increase public sector employment do not provide the easy way out so often thought.

As indicated in earlier chapters, although the government largely abandoned 'monetarism' early on in its first term of office,[19] it kept to its resolve to bring about a decline in the rate of growth money GDP, consistent with a progressive decline in the inflation rate. Rightly, it resisted pressure to allow nominal money demand to grow at a faster

19 Although the government still (1987) 'targets' MO growth, the main purpose appears to be to monitor the growth of money GDP.

rate, relying on a declining rate of growth of money wages and incomes to permit faster growth of output. But would it have been more sensible – and indeed possible – to exert a more direct restraint on money wages in the hope of achieving a faster growth of output and a faster fall in unemployment?

Of course, incomes policies have been tried in the UK on a number of occasions without much long term success (see chapter 1); nonetheless they remain attractive to many otherwise liberal economists since analytically they appear to overcome the so-called 'prisoners' dilemma' characteristic of pay bargaining. The essence of this is that while it can be shown that if *everybody* pursues wage restraint the community will be better off than if they didn't (i.e. there will be less need to deflate the economy), it is in the rational interests of each individual or individual group to prefer higher pay settlements irrespective of the behaviour of other individuals or groups. If all other individuals or groups accept pay restraint, there are clear gains for the one who didn't; if all others did not accept pay restraint, there would be greater loss for the one who did. Thus individual rationality can breed aggregate or communal irrationality. The strength of an incomes policy is that it provides some assurance to the individual or an individual group that all other individuals or groups will pursue wage restraint when he or it does. The weakness however is obvious: it is still rational for each individual or group to break the pay norm in the hope that others won't.

Thus there are two necessary conditions for a traditional incomes policy to succeed: first, pay bargainers must be confident that a settlement above the incomes policy norm will trigger equally high settlements elsewhere, and second, that this will leave their group of workers worse off (because of the resulting rise in the general price level) than if the norm had not been breached. These conditions are hardly ever satisfied; indeed, given that incomes policies have usually been introduced when inflation is getting out of hand, and have generally been accompanied by macroeconomic policy measures to restrain aggregate demand, there has been strong incentive for all to break the norm, since the share of wages in national output will, at least temporarily, tend to rise.

The establishment of a statutory incomes policy requires trade union consent and co-operation; and in the UK this has generally been obtained only at a high price. Union leaders have usually insisted on wages being fully indexed to future price increases, so guaranteeing no loss of real income. They have often insisted on complementary measures to constrain profits, so ensuring that the wage share in value added did not fall: more often than not the share tended to rise as profits were squeezed. Moreover, unions have generally insisted on macro-policies aimed at maintaining full employment regardless of productivity and efficiency. Whilst such policies and conditions were possibly tenable in the 1950s and early 1960s, worsening terms of trade caused first by currency devaluation and then by the 1973-4 oil price shock inevitably meant a fall in the real wage (relative to labour productivity) at which full employment could be obtained. The indexing of money wages after 1973 greatly exacerbated the inflationary shock of the oil price rise, and despite the expansionary fiscal and monetary policies that were pursued, ensured that unemployment would also rise.

Despite the inherent weaknesses of incomes policies and the UK's unfortunate experience with them in the 1970s, the seriousness of the unemployment problem in the UK has maintained widespread support for them, albeit in new or modified forms. A new proposal, aimed directly at the employment problem, has been put forward by Professor J.E. Meade.[20] This bows towards the monetarist position by proposing that monetary policy should remain the principal determinant of the growth of nominal income; but in order to ensure that nominal income growth is associated with real output and employment growth rather than price increases, it proposes that wage settlements be subject to some form of arbitration process. Wage settlements which are agreed between employees and employers (or their representatives) should go through without interruption, but those which are not agreed should be referred to an arbitration process. The overriding criterion applied here would be whether, given the target growth for nominal national income, the disputed wage settlement would be conducive to increasing the level of employment. There would be no national norm and no maximum, and local factors could be allowed for.

Although rightly directed at the major problem - unemployment, rather than inflation - there are many difficulties. Since referral to arbitration is not to be compulsory, what happens if employers or employees refuse to co-operate? Is the government simply to be regarded as an ordinary employer, with powers to refer disputes to arbitration? Suppose the arbitration award was not accepted by one or other of both parties? The award could be made binding on employers, as Professor Meade suggests, but then measures (such as reducing legal immunities) would be required to weaken the bargaining strength of employees and unions - a course of action which the present

20 J.E. Meade, *Stagflation, vol. 1: Wage Fixing* (Allen and Unwin, London, 1982).

government is already embarked on, although not without opposition.

Practical problems are associated with all types of incomes policies. How, for example, to deal with productivity increases? If loopholes are not to be created in the system, adjustments may well have to be made retrospectively, possibly creating problems at the macroeconomic level. How to define particular groups for bargaining purposes, given different skills and different regional unemployment situations? It is not surprising that the present government has shown considerable reluctance to embark on incomes policies, particularly when the trade union movement as a whole has affirmed its outright opposition to any of its forms.

The administrative nightmare associated with traditional incomes policies (even with the policy proposed by Professor Meade which aims at the right objective – namely, employment rather than at inflation) has stimulated the search for other approaches to the problem. One that has obtained support from at least one of the political parties (the late SDP) is due to Professor Layard.[21] This proposes that the government should levy a tax on employers who award their employees an increase in earnings above a fixed norm. The amount of the tax could be a percentage (perhaps 100 per cent) of the excess increase above the norm. Flexibility in pay setting would not be reduced since it would not be unlawful for firms to pay above the norm, but the firm could not ignore the impact of the tax on its profits and performance. Strong downwards pressure on excess wage growth would be created.

Of course, the tax could be passed on to the consumer in higher prices so that the government would have to have a target growth rate for nominal national income – and be ready to enforce it through fiscal or monetary policy – for the potential inflationary impact of the tax to be restrained. It might also discourage productivity increases or overtime working – which, although perhaps good for employment, is not necessarily good for national economic performance or competitiveness. Since for administrative reasons the application of the tax would have to be confined to larger companies – firms employing more than 100 workers – and since the ability to pass on the tax to consumers would differ from firm to firm, friction could be created between firms. Those firms losing out might mobilize themselves to resist the policy. Finally, since it would be absurd of the government to tax its own enterprises – nationalized industries and public sector departments – in order to discourage them from awarding excess pay

21 See R. Layard and S. Nickell, *An Incomes Policy to help the Unemployed* (Employment Institute, Nov. 1986).

increases, one of the main sources of inflationary wage pressure would be left out. Nonetheless, in so far as the tax successfully restrained inflationary pressure from the supply side, less responsibility would be imposed on demand side policies, with probable benefit to output and employment. So far, however, the difficulty of fixing an appropriate norm, and the danger that productivity and efficiency would be discouraged, have constituted sufficient grounds for the government to reject it as an un-tried scheme.

In the end the question becomes one of whether administrative or tax-based incomes policies really get to grips with the problem facing the British economy and its labour markets. In the view of some critics of the Thatcher government,[22] they do not, and a far more fundamental attack is suggested, namely, the abolition of collective bargaining between unions and employers. Since this would mean in effect a major attack on the legal immunity of trade unions from tort action, as well as application of the Monopoly Commission's brief to the ability of the unions to regulate and restrict supply of labour, it would be deemed political dynamite.

The theoretical case against collective bargaining is the same as the case against all forms of monopoly control, namely that by restricting supply and raising price a monopolist can obtain greater total utility than if he sets price lower and output higher. In the case of a trade union, where the utility maximizer is a collection of individuals, action to raise the money wage above the competitive level implies that some of those individuals will lose out, by becoming unemployed; while those who keep their jobs benefit from the higher money wages obtained. In the UK as in all modern industrial countries, the losers are protected to some extent by the safety net of unemployment pay and other social security benefits. Without such benefits trade union leaders would clearly have less power, for they would be faced with the opposition of those of their members who would lose out. But given such benefits, losers effectively disenfranchise themselves from the labour force and are no longer the concern of union leaders. In the terms used earlier, outsiders are created whose interests are ignored in future wage bargaining by the insiders.

In a paper on labour market competition, Beenstock and Minford have collected evidence to show that collective bargaining has raised money wages above the competitive (i.e. non-unionized) level in the

22 For example, M. Beenstock and P. Minford, 'Curing Unemployment through Labour Market Competition', *Monetarism and Macro-economics*, Institute of Economic Affairs, 1987.

UK by something like 10 per cent. They have also shown on evidence taken from Layard, Metcalf and Nickell that union mark-up above the competitive level has tended to rise throughout the post-war period up to 1980.[23] Econometric analysis of the data suggests that the real value of social security benefits and the extent of union membership in the labour force have played an important role. As might be expected, the mark-up is anticyclical, varying directly with the rate of unemployment – i.e. unions have been successful in protecting their members' relative wage position in recession, presumably at the expense of employment.

Beenstock and Minford see further support for their contention that trade union power has been a major cause of growing unemployment in the UK (and Europe) compared with the very different circumstances of the US. The relative moderation in real wage growth in the US compared to what happened in the UK and Europe has been referred to earlier in this chapter, as has been the very different behaviour of employment and unemployment. In Beenstock and Minford's view the different behaviour of real wages and therefore of employment reflects the high degree of unionization in the UK and Europe compared with the US (see table 6.8). Moreover, whereas in the UK and Europe union wages tended to have a mark-up of at least 10 per cent on non-union wages, there has typically been very little difference in the US.

The Beenstock and Minford view has had a sympathetic hearing by the Thatcher administration, which has taken a number of steps,

**Table 6.8**   Proportion of workers belonging to trade unions

|        | *US\** | *W. Germany* | *Belgium* | *UK* |
|--------|--------|--------------|-----------|------|
| 1960   | 31.4   | 37.2         | 62.0      | 43.1 |
| 1965   | 28.4   | 36.0         | 63.0      | 43.2 |
| 1970   | 27.0   | 35.8         | 68.9      | 50.9 |
| 1975   | 24.5   | 39.2         | 75.8      | 53.7 |
| 1980   | 25.2   | 40.3         | 77.3      | 56.4 |
| 1984   | 18.8   | 41.5         | n.a.      | 53.9 |

[a] Excludes agricultural workers and includes the unemployed in the denominator.
*Source*: M. Beenstock and P. Minford, 'Curing Unemployment through Labour Market Competition', *Monetarism and Macro-economics*, Institute for Economic Affairs, 1987.

23  Beenstock and Minford, 'Curing Unemployment', table 1 and fig. 2.

(described in chapter 4), to weaken the power of trade unions in the UK. But while the legislation that has been carried through has undoubtedly weakened the power of unions to maintain restrictive practices and has therefore promoted the more efficient use of labour, it has not affected the power of the unions to determine pay: legislation preserves the power of unions to resort to strike action to support pay claims if backed by their members. Thus Beenstock and Minford contend that the net effect of the legislation has been to increase unemployment: trade unions have been unable to prevent redundancies and layoffs due to better working practices and higher productivity but they have prevented the necessary wage flexibility that would have led to job creation. While restraints on closed shops and union secondary action will encourage the growth of non-union firms and in the long run promote employment, the short run effect has undoubtedly been negative for employment.

The implication of Beenstock and Minford's analysis is that the 1906 Trade Union Act, which gave the trade unions immunity from tort actions, should be repealed and that the unions should not be above the common law. The unions would be compelled to negotiate contracts that were enforceable in law. Damages could then be claimed in the case of non-fulfillment. If at the same time the exercise of trade union monopoly could be subject to Monopoly Commission investigation, trade union power to force inflation and/or unemployment would be greatly curtailed.

Despite the theoretical and practical force of Beenstock and Minford's attack on the governments' limited attempts to pair down the power of trade unions and create a more flexible labour market, it seems doubtful whether the appropriate political climate existed or exists today to carry out the far reaching reforms proposed. There would have to be at least as far reaching constraints on the power of firms to fix prices and constrain competition. Moreover, given the heavy structural unemployment affecting many parts of the country – which admittedly has been promoted by past trade union determination and power to resist change – and given also severe constraints on labour mobility imposed by long term housing policy, it seems most unlikely that unemployment would have been greatly reduced. Although government has to avoid repeating the mistakes of the past, these can hardly be eliminated in the space of a few years.

While slow to recognize the failure of the labour market to behave in the classical way (i.e. equilibrate the demand for and supply of labour through flexible wages) but rightly unwilling to embark on Keynesian demand expansion that would prejudice a decline in inflation, the

**Table 6.9** Major government schemes to assist the unemployed and young workers in operation since 1983

| | Date of opening (if after Apr. 1983) | Date of closing (if appropriate) | Declared objective(s) | Major condition(s)/comments |
|---|---|---|---|---|
| Enterprise and job creation | | | | |
| Enterprise Allowance Scheme | Aug. 1983 (national scheme) | | To assist unemployed and redundant workers to set up business on their own account | £40 p.w. for one year. Entrepreneurs need access to £1,000 |
| Labour market efficiency | | | | |
| Restart | Apr. 1987 (national scheme) | | To provide special counselling for those unemployed for six months or longer to help them return to work | Counselling interviews can lead for example to job interviews, a Job Start Allowance of £20 p.w. for full-time jobs of less than £80 p.w., a Community Programme place, Jobclub membership or a Restart course |

| Scheme | Date | Purpose | Details |
|---|---|---|---|
| **Labour mobility** June 1986 Travel to Interview Scheme Employment Transfer Scheme Job Search Scheme Free Forward Fares Scheme | 1986 | To encourage unemployed people to seek jobs in other areas by helping with interview expenses | |
| **Employment measures** Community Programme | | To provide temporary work and training opportunities for long-term unemployed adults on projects of benefit to the community | Current average wage £67 p.w. |
| Community Industry | | Temporary employment for particularly disadvantaged young people | Age 17–19 |
| Job Release Scheme (Full-time) Job Release Scheme (Part-time) | May 1986 | Allows an older person to retire early by payment of a weekly allowance provided a job is released which is filled by an unemployed person | Mainly men aged 64 and women aged 59 |

**Table 6.9** *continued*

| | Date of opening (if after Apr. 1983) | Date of closing (if appropriate) | Declared objective(s) | Major condition(s)/ comments |
|---|---|---|---|---|
| Job Splitting Scheme | Jan. 1983 | | To encourage more flexible working arrangements by, for example, splitting a full-time job into two part-time ones | |
| Temporary Short-Time Working Compensation Scheme | | Mar. 1984 | To encourage short-time working instead of redundancy | |
| Voluntary Projects Programme | | | To generate opportunities for the unemployed to undertake voluntary activities which develop skills | |
| Young Workers Scheme | Sept. 1983 | Mar. 1986 | Programme of training and work experience for young people | 17 year olds at a gross average wage of £50 p.w. |

| Scheme | Date | Description | Age/Details |
|---|---|---|---|
| New Workers Scheme | Apr. 1986 | Complements Youth Training Scheme (see below) by helping employers take on 18–20 year olds at wages which reflect youth and inexperience | 18–20 year olds. Maximum wage of £55 p.w. (£65 p.w. for 20 year olds) |
| Training Youth Training Scheme 2 Year YTS | Sept. 1983 Apr. 1986 | From 1986 provides two year structured work experience and training to 16 year old school leavers and one year for 17 year old school leavers | 16–17 year olds |
| Job Training Scheme | Apr. 1987 (national scheme) | To offer unemployed young people about six months training | |

**Table 6.9** *continued*

| | Date of opening (if after Apr. 1983) | Date of closing (if appropriate) | Declared objective(s) | Major condition(s)/ comments |
|---|---|---|---|---|
| Adult training Training Opportunities Scheme Job Training Programme Wider Opportunities Training | | 1985 | To meet national and local skill needs and to help the employed, unemployed, self-employed and employers to enhance their skills | A wide range of schemes |
| Programme Open Tech/Open learning | 1985 | | | |
| Technical and Vocational Education Initiative | Sept. 1984 (expansion) Autumn 1987 (national scheme) | | To provide technical and vocational education for 14–18 year olds | 14–18 year olds |
| Non-Advanced Further Education | | | To increase the responsiveness of local authority provision to labour market needs | |

*Source:* Public Expenditure White Papers (PEWP), 1983–7

government took energetic steps of a microeconomic kind in its second term of office to mitigate the unemployment situation. A myriad of schemes were introduced after 1983, some aimed at the long term unemployed, others at younger workers, particularly school leavers, divided broadly between employment creating measures and training. They range from schemes aimed at assisting redundant workers to set up business on their own account, to programmes for providing counselling, training and work experience for 17 year olds (see tables 6.9 and 6.10). The number of workers covered by the schemes amounted to over 700,000 in 1986. In addition, the government has plans, starting in 1987, to provide special counselling services for over a million of the long term unemployed and financial assistance to enable them to take low paid jobs.

Nonetheless, although the training facilities offered to younger workers should have beneficial long term implications for their future job prospects, these schemes are unlikely to solve Britain's long term unemployment problem. Although providing short term relief, they cannot provide the more permanent jobs required by the unemployed. The peculiar regional concentration of unemployment in the UK would also seem to indicate a need for more closely targeted measures that would directly increase the demand for labour in the afflicted areas, and there is no shortage of suggestions. A scheme proposed by Professor Layard, for example, is that marginal job subsidies should be paid to private employers who increase their total employment in designated regions.[24] In addition, the government could vary rates of employers' National Insurance contributions – a not insignificant element in labour costs – lowering them in areas of high long term unemployment and raising them in areas of strong labour demand. Moreover, the creation of new jobs in particularly afflicted areas could be completely exempted from employer contributions, at least until the situation was improving. Of course, such schemes as these can involve large 'deadweight' costs – viz. the cost of subsidies or forgiven taxes and insurance contributions on labour that would have been employed anyway. Also there is the danger that employment could simply be shifted from one firm to another and/or from one area to another, little or no net increase in employment being achieved. However, lowering labour costs at the margin relative to the cost of capital could lead to the substitution of labour for capital (or perhaps, more realistically, inhibit the substitution the other way).

24 R. Layard, *How to Beat Unemployment* (Oxford University Press 1986).

**Table 6.10** Numbers covered by government sponsored schemes to assist the unemployed and young workers (thousands)

| | 1983/4 | 1984/5 | 1985/6 | 1986/7[a] | 1987/8 Plan | 1988/9 Plan | 1989/90 Plan |
|---|---|---|---|---|---|---|---|
| **Enterprise and job creation** | | | | | | | |
| Enterprise Allowance Scheme[b] | 25[a] | 35[a] | 60 | 86 | 110[c] | 110[c] | 110[c] |
| **Labour market efficiency** | | | | | | | |
| Restart[f] | – | – | 14[a] | 1,360[g] | 700[g] | 700[g] | 700[g] |
| of which Job Start Allowance | – | – | 0.1 | 8 | 20 | 20 | 20 |
| **Labour mobility** | | | | | | | |
| Travel to Interview Scheme | – | – | – | – | 17.2 | n.a. | n.a. |
| Employment Transfer Scheme | 3.8 | 3.3 | 3.8[a] | n.a. | – | – | – |
| Job Search Scheme | 4.1 | 4.3 | 6.6 | – | – | – | – |
| Free Forward Fares Scheme | 9.6 | 9.3 | 11.3 | – | – | – | – |
| **Employment measures[d]** | | | | | | | |
| Community Programme | 106 | 126 | 159 | 241 | 245[c] | 245[e] | 245[e] |
| Community Industry | 8 | 8 | 8 | 8 | 8 | 8 | 8 |
| Job Release Scheme (Full-time) | 86 | 84 | 52 | 68 | 26[e] | 27[e] | 26[e] |
| Job Release Scheme (Part-time) | n.a. | 0.2 | 0.2 | – | – | – | – |
| Job Splitting Scheme | 0.7 | 0.2 | 0.3 | 0.3 | 1[e] | 1[e] | 1[e] |
| Temporary Short-Time Working Compensation Scheme | 29 | – | – | – | – | – | – |
| Voluntary Projects Programme | n.a. | 12.4 | 14 | 15[c] | 14[e] | 14[e] | 14[e] |
| New Workers Scheme | – | – | – | 0.3 | 50[e] | 72[e] | 77[e] |
| Young Workers Scheme | 107 | 71 | 54 | 24 | 1[e] | – | – |

| Training | | | | | | |
|---|---|---|---|---|---|---|
| Youth Training Scheme | 350 | 350[a] | 364 | 362 | 362[g] | 346[g] | 321[g] |
| Technical and Vocational Education Initiative | n.a. | n.a. | 40 | 61 | 80 | – | – |
| Adult Training | | | | | | | |
| Training Opportunities Scheme | 80[a] | 81[a] | – | – | – | – | – |
| Job Training Programme | – | – | 183 | 197 | 285[g] | 401[g] | n.a.[g] |
| Wider Opportunities Training Programme | – | – | 55 | 45 | 38 | 33 | 33 |
| Open Tech/Open Learning | n.a. | n.a. | 32 | 50 | n.a. | n.a. | n.a. |
| Non-Advanced Further Education | – | – | – | – | – | – | – |

[a] Estimate.
[b] End-year.
[c] Includes 10 % increase announced Jan. 1987.
[d] October.
[e] March.
[f] Numbers counselled.
[g] To be increased as a result of measures announced in Jan. 1987.

*Source*: National Economic Development Office, *The British Labour Market and Unemployment* (NEDC, 1987), 16, annexe 1

addition to targeted measures of the kind described above, there is
ous scope for public works of a labour intensive kind. If coupled
1 measures to encourage contractors to engage long term unem-
yed labour, a significant dent could be made in the number unemployed, subject to the reservations made earlier in this chapter.

## The Record

How should we summarize the Thatcher government's record on
unemployment? It is clear that macroeconomic policy, particularly in
1979–81, was responsible in a proximate sense for a substantial part of
the rise in unemployment; but it is also clear that the basis for this had
been well and truly laid in the 1970s by Britain's appalling productivity
performance. Britain's manufacturing industry could not remain for
ever in the overmanned, low productivity state which a combination
of the irresponsible exercise of trade union power and government
obsession with maintaining full employment had left it: at some stage,
a huge labour shake-out was inevitable.[25] The resulting unemployment was not of the kind that could respond to Keynesian demand
expansion – and the government was rightly concerned to pull down
inflation – but nor could it be handled by leaving it to the classical
working of the labour market. Although, given the high inflation and
large budget deficit it had inherited from the previous administration,
the government could be excused for not embarking immediately on
expensive microeconomic measures that would be needed to contract
structural and regional unemployment, the delay in introducing them
undoubtedly consolidated the problem. While the wide range of
employment and training schemes introduced after 1983 has been
welcome, they cannot in themselves provide long term employment
opportunities in the most affected areas. Moreover the government's
reluctance to grasp the housing nettle (which is a severe constraint on
labour mobility), while politically understandable, makes it more difficult for unemployment to be dealt with. Nonetheless, it is not without
significance that the very rapid growth of the UK economy during
1986–7 was associated with a fall in unemployment which by the

25 It is interesting to note that the increase in real GDP between 1979 and
1985 was little different from the increase in the years 1973-9 under the
Labour government, especially if allowance is made for the miners' strike.
What was very different was the behaviour of employment and
unemployment relative to output.

autumn of 1987 had declined to well below 3 million (table 6.1).

Even so, it is evident that the UK suffers from an endemic labour market problem which renders the short term trade-off between inflation and unemployment very high and which, in the long term, appears to condemn the country to a high level of unemployment irrespective of inflation. An important element in this is the failure of the UK's educational system to meet the skill and other needs required of a modern industrial labour force – but the seeds of this go back well in time. Indeed, it can well be argued that Britain's short term problems – inflation and unemployment – are less the result of the short term macroeconomic policies pursued than of long term deficiencies in the economy that have only slowly been recognized. If this is the case, assessment of Thatcher policies must go beyond their apparent short term results and must look instead at how far the deep-rooted malaise in the economy has been affected.

# 7

# An Overall Assessment

Critical assessment of economic policy and performance of the British economy under Mrs Thatcher has largely centred on the high level of unemployment which has been associated with it. For good measure, 'the destruction of UK manufacturing industry' and 'the waste of North Sea oil' are thrown in, and, despite increased spending in real as well as monetary terms, 'attack on the welfare state' is often included. However, if attention is focused on the long term and underlying problems of the UK described in chapter 1, and on the factors listed by Corelli Barnett as contributing to them,[1] it could well be argued that the Thatcher government's refusal to maintain full employment at any cost in terms of low productivity, low efficiency, high inflation; its refusal to maintain the welfare state at any cost in terms of resource use; and its refusal to maintain uneconomic industry for the sake of maintaining employment in depressed areas of the economy do not *per se* constitute evidence of mistaken policy or policy failure: on the contrary, the evidence might indicate that the UK's long term economic problems were at last being tackled.

Indeed as a statement of the case for focusing attention along these lines the following extract from a speech by Mr Callaghan (who became prime minister of the Labour government in 1976) can hardly be bettered:

> For too long, perhaps ever since the war, we postponed facing up to fundamental choices and fundamental changes in our society and in our economy. That is what I mean when I say we have been living on borrowed time. For too long this country . . . has been ready to settle

1 Corelli Barnett, *The Audit of War* (Macmillan, London 1986).

for borrowing money abroad to maintain our standards of life, instead of grappling with the fundamental problem of British industry . . .

We used to think that you could spend your way out of a recession and increase employment by cutting taxes and boosting government spending.

I tell you in all candour that the option no longer exists, and that in so far as it ever did exist, it only worked on each occasion since the war by injecting a bigger dose of inflation into the economy, followed by a higher level of unemployment as the next step. Higher inflation followed by higher unemployment. We have just escaped from the highest rate of inflation this country has known; we have not yet escaped from the consequences: high unemployment. That is the history of the last twenty years.[2]

Thus, from this point of view, the real test of the Thatcher policy would be not whether it has adhered to the post-war aim of full employment but whether it has brought about, or at least set the scene for, improvement in Britain's longer term economic performance. Although, given the deep rooted nature of those problems, overnight change can hardly be expected, eight years seems a long enough period for at least some signs to manifest themselves. In fact there are such signs, particularly in the greatly improved productivity performance of British industry in recent years, which suggest that a real and much needed transformation has taken place and can bode well for the future.

### Signs of Revival

Although the definition and measurement of productivity is beset with a host of problems, necessitating extreme care when conclusions are drawn,[3] there is general agreement that a substantial improvement has occurred in the last few years, not only as compared with the 1970s – a particularly disastrous period – but also as compared with the 1960s, particularly if total factor productivity is the measure:[4] see tables 7.1, 7.2 and 7.3.

2 James Callaghan, *Time and Chance* (Collins, London, 1987).

3 For a discussion of the problems and pitfalls of measuring productivity and its growth, see John Muellbauer, 'The assessment: productivity and competitiveness in British manufacturing', *Oxford Review of Economic Policy*, 2/3 (Autumn 1986).

4 Total factor productivity is a measure of changes in output that cannot be explained by labour hours worked, employment levels, and changes in the measured capital stock.

**Table 7.1**    Output per head of the employed labour force

|  | 1964–73 | 1973–9 | 1979–86 (first half) |
|---|---|---|---|
|  | (Average annual % change) | | |
| Manufacturing | 3.8 | 0.7 | 3.8 |
| Non-manufacturing[a] | 2.9 | 0.6 | 1.2 |
| Whole economy | 2.7 | 1.1 | 1.9 |

[a] Excluding public services and North Seal oil and gas.
*Source*: *Economic Progress Report* (HM Treasury), 188 (Jan.–Feb. 1987)

**Table 7.2**    UK manufacturing: total factor productivity

| | |
|---|---|
| 1956 (first quarter) to 1959 (third quarter) | 1.7 % p.a. |
| 1959 (fourth quarter) to 1972 (fourth quarter) | 2.63% p.a. |
| 1973 (first quarter) to 1979 (second quarter) | 0.62% p.a. |
| 1979 (third quarter) to 1980 (second quarter) | – 1.93% p.a. |
| 1980 (third quarter) to 1985 (fourth quarter) | 2.76% p.a. |

*Source*: Muellbauer, 'The assessment: productivity and competitiveness in British manufacturing', *Oxford Review of Economic Policy*, 2/3 (Autumn 1986)

**Table 7.3**    Productivity trends in UK manufacturing (% increase per annum

|  | (1) Total factor productivity | (2) Substitution effect | (1) + (2) Labour productivity |
|---|---|---|---|
| 1956 (first quarter) to 1959 (third quarter) | 1.71 | 1.42 | 3.13 |
| 1959 (fourth quarter) to 1972 (fourth quarter) | 2.63 | 1.54 | 4.17 |
| 1973 (first quarter) to 1979 (second quarter) | 0.62 | 1.21 | 1.83 |
| 1979 (third quarter) to 1980 (second quarter) | – 1.93 | 2.03 | 0.10 |
| 1980 (third quarter) to 1986 (fourth quarter) | 3.17 | 1.77 | 4.84 |

*Source*: P. Spencer, *Britain's Productivity Renaissance* (Crédit Suisse/First Boston Securities, June 1987)

Labour productivity fell sharply during the recession of 1979–80 when manufacturing output showed its largest fall in the post-war period; but from the end of 1980 it started to rise even though output was still falling, and it continued to rise at a fast rate during the next five years when output was also rising. Even allowing for the recession of 1979–80, labour productivity in manufacturing rose by 3.8 per cent per annum from 1979 to the first half of 1986, as compared with less than 1 per cent per annum in the previous six years (see table 7.1). Excluding 1979–80, productivity performance at close to 5 per cent per annum was probably better than at any time in the previous twenty years. Labour productivity in non-manufacturing and therefore in the economy as a whole did less well (2 per cent per annum) although still better than in the second half of the 1970s. Muellbauer's work suggests that total factor productivity (i.e. changes in output that cannot be explained by labour hours worked, by changes in employment levels, or by changes in the *measured* capital stock) also rose faster in the years 1980–5 than at any time during the previous 25 years (see table 7.2).

Indeed, Muellbauer, probably no ardent supporter of Thatcherism, after careful analysis of the data concludes that the improvement in productivity growth in Britain after the end of 1980 was remarkable and that the sheer steadiness of growth over six years cannot be explained simply by the shedding of the low productivity tail of Britain's manufacturing sector: the better-than-average performers must also have done much better.

Muellbauer's estimates have been revised by P. Spencer on the basis of subsequent revisions to data relating to manufacturing output and employment (the former having been raised and the latter lowered since Muellbauer's original work for the period up to 1985) and also to include an extra year 1986. Spencer concludes that since the third quarter of 1980 total factor productivity has risen by 3.17 per cent per annum and labour productivity at 4.84 per cent per annum – a performance that far exceeds anything witnessed in the earlier post-war period (see table 7.3). In fact, helped by a strong rise in manufacturing output, labour productivity increased at an annual rate of near 7 per cent through 1987–8.

Equally striking is the improved British productivity performance relative to other major industrialized countries (see table 7.4). In the twenty years prior to 1979, the UK's productivity performance in both manufacturing and the whole economy, lay at the bottom or next to bottom of the league table, and of course well below average performance of the group as a whole. Since 1979, however, output per head

**Table 7.4** Output per head in the major seven industrialized countries (average annual % change)

|  | Manufacturing | | | Whole economy | | |
|---|---|---|---|---|---|---|
|  | 1960–70 | 1970–80 | 1980–8 (first half) | 1960–70 | 1970–80 | 1980–8 (first half) |
| United States | 3.5 | 3.0 | 4.0 | 2.0 | 0.4 | 1.2 |
| Japan | 8.8 | 5.3 | 3.1 | 8.9 | 3.8 | 2.9 |
| West Germany | 4.1 | 2.9 | 2.2 | 4.4 | 2.8 | 1.8 |
| France[a] | 5.4 | 3.2 | 3.1 | 4.6 | 2.8 | 2.0 |
| UK | 3.0 | 1.6 | 5.2 | 2.4 | 1.3 | 2.5 |
| Italy[a] | 5.4 | 3.0 | 3.5 | 6.3 | 2.6 | 2.0 |
| Canada | 3.4 | 3.0 | 3.6 | 2.4 | 1.5 | 1.4 |
| Average of major seven[b] | 4.5 | 3.3 | 3.6 | 3.5 | 1.7 | 1.8 |

[a] For whole industry, not just manufacturing.
[b] Weighted on basis of 1980 manufacturing output, at 1980 exchange rates.
*Source: Economic Progress Report* (HM Treasury), 201 (April 1989).

in manufacturing industry has increased at a faster rate than in any other major industrial country, and in the whole economy at a rate inferior only to that of Japan. Thus there is some evidence that a sea change has taken place in the British economy, even though the relative improvement as compared with the decade of 1970s is somewhat exaggerated – since performance in this decade was as in all other countries, adversely affected by oil price shocks which not only checked output growth but also led to the substitution of labour and capital for energy and consequently a decline in productivity.

It seems clear that an improvement in productivity which has been sustained for so long and shows every sign of continuing must be explained in terms of at least some of the longer term and fundamental factors typically underlying productivity growth: improved management, better working practices, better directed investment, and greater readiness to change. The improved performance seems to be spread over most sectors of British manufacturing industry, being particularly marked in the metals, motor-car manufacturing and electrical engineering sectors of the economy (see table 7.5). Indeed, the improve-

**Table 7.5**  Output, jobs, productivity 1979–86: % change ( + or – )

| | Since first half of 1979 | | | Since first quarter of 1981 | | |
|---|---|---|---|---|---|---|
| | Output | Jobs | Output per head | Output | Jobs | Output per head |
| Metals | – 11.1 | – 56.0 | + 102.0 | + 16.8 | – 39.2 | + 90.8 |
| Motors, parts | – 30.2 | – 47.9 | + 34.0 | + 11.9 | – 33.8 | + 69.0 |
| Electrical engineering | + 29.6 | – 21.0 | + 64.1 | + 44.7 | – 13.9 | + 68.1 |
| Mechanical engineering | – 16.6 | – 30.8 | 20.5 | + 5.1 | – 23.3 | + 37.0 |
| Chemicals | + 13.9 | – 14.9 | + 33.8 | + 27.0 | – 4.7 | + 33.3 |
| Textiles | – 19.2 | – 38.6 | + 31.6 | + 11.3 | – 16.4 | + 33.1 |
| Paper, print | – 3.1 | – 6.6 | + 3.7 | + 9.1 | – 1.9 | + 11.2 |
| All manufacturing | – 3.9 | – 28.0 | + 33.5 | + 13.9 | – 17.9 | + 38.7 |

*Source*: *Economic Progress Report* (HM Treasury), 189 (Mar.–Apr. 1989)

ments in some key sectors of the economy have been dramatic. For example, British Steel, which in the 1970s was the most inefficient steel producer in Europe, with labour productivity 40 per cent below that in Germany, has achieved a rate of production which is now on a par with that in Germany. Whereas each tonne of steel took an average of 14.5 hours to produce in 1980–1, by the last quarter of 1986 it was taking only 5.6 hours. British Steel's enormous financial losses of the 1970s have been turned into profits.[5] The British car industry, virtually destroyed in the 1970s by anarchic industrial relations and by frequent strikes, is now very much in the ascendant. Productivity in some plants has more than doubled, bringing it up to Continental standards. According to one expert on the automobile industry, Professor Garel Rhys, 'Britain is becoming a highly efficient place to manufacture cars. The underlying productivity is as high as anything on the Continent'.[6] Undoubtedly, although the dramatic fall in strikes, both official and unofficial, and in work stoppages has been a major factor in the car industry's greater productivity, improved technology, made possible by better industrial relations, has been at least as important.

5 'Industry's miracle revival' and 'Where a strike's just a memory', *Sunday Times*, 8 Feb. 1987.
6 'Britain's car industry starts motoring again', *Sunday Times*, 18 Feb. 1987.

There is a temptation to play down Britain's greatly improved industrial performance in the 1980s by noting that in those sectors where productivity has risen most – metals and car manufacturing, for example – output has fallen as compared with 1979 (although not, of course, as compared with 1981), and employment has fallen massively. There is a temptation to conclude that jobs have been lost for nothing. Some observers even go so far as to suggest that the productivity growth is no more than an illusion, since if employment had not fallen, recorded productivity would have shown a fall rather than a rise.[7] Of course it cannot be disputed that an enormous shake-out of labour occurred in the 1980s, particularly in the sharp downturn during 1979–81. Equally, it cannot be disputed that much of British industry was afflicted by massive overmanning in the 1960s and 1970s, making it inevitable that if the UK was ever to compete with other countries at real wages acceptable to the British worker, a massive shake-out had to occur. Moreover, it is quite illegitimate to assume that output could have been maintained through the 1980s at unchanged levels of employment without the massive underlying rise in labour productivity that in fact occurred. Given the slow-down in world economic activity and the intense international competition that existed, a substantial fall in real wages in UK manufacturing industry would have been required in order to maintain both output and employment at 1979 levels.

Further evidence of the improvement in UK manufacturing productivity and efficiency can be found in the behaviour of profits. As indicated in chapter 1, the decade of the 1970s was characterized by a steep fall in the rate of profit on capital employed in manufacturing industry. By the end of the decade it had reached the abysmally low level of barely 5 per cent. After 1981 it rose markedly, to over 8 per cent (although in 1986 it was still lower than it had been at the end of the 1960s) – (see figure 7.1). Taking all industrial and commercial companies together, excluding North Sea oil, the net real rate of return on capital employed had recovered to over 14 per cent in 1987, compared with less than 7 per cent in 1979. However, despite the absolute and relative improvement in UK manufacturing productivity during 1981–6, output per hour in 1987 remained substantially lower than in most of the country's main industrial competitors (see table 7.6). The best that can be said is that the UK has moved up in the league, and much remains to be done. For this reason, the outlook for employment in manufacturing is clearly rather bleak (see later).

Can the undoubted absolute and relative improvement in Britain's

7 David Smith, 'Productivity alone no guarantee of success', *The Times*, 18 Feb. 1987.

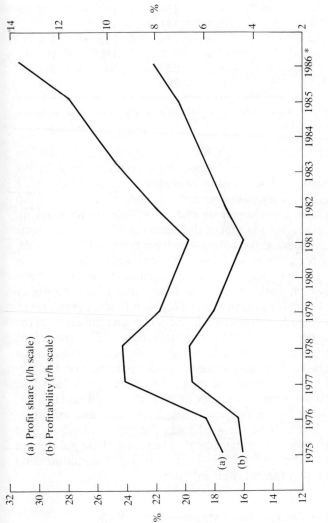

Gross operating surplus as % of (a) Value added, (b) Gross capital stock

\*CFSB estimates

**Figure 7.1** The profitability of UK manufacturing industry

*Source:* P. Spencer, *Britain's Productivity Renaissance* (Crédit Suisse First Boston Securities, June 1987)

uitation‎

**Table 7.6**  Labour productivity (output per hour: UK = 100)

|  | 1980 | 1984 | 1986 |
|---|---|---|---|
| United States | 273 | 262 | 267 |
| Japan | 196 | 177 | 176 |
| France | 193 | 179 | 184 |
| Germany | 255 | 232 | 178 |
| Italy | 173 | 156 | 155 |
| Belgium | 207 | 200 | 154 |
| Netherlands | 269 | 267 | 205 |

*Source*: G.F. Ray, 'Labour Costs in Manufacturing', *National Institute Economic Review*, May 1987

productivity performance, which has nevertheless taken place, be ascribed in any specific way to the economic policy pursued by the Thatcher government? There would probably be general agreement that the government's legislative attack on trade union power and privilege (summarized in chapter 4) and its willingness to stand up against crucial strikes (such as that of the miners in 1984), or to provide explicit or implicit support for others who have done so (for example, during the the printers' strike of 1986–7), have played a significant role in reducing trade union opposition to the introduction of new technology and to changes in working practices. Many, including some highly critical of other aspects of government policy, would rate the reform of industrial relations and the reduction in the power and influence of the trade unions as the government's biggest success: 'The spectre of Britain being ungovernable without union consent . . . may at last have been banished'.[8] But there is perhaps less agreement on the precise part played by macroeconomic policy *per se*, except perhaps that the government's willingness to accept or (as some would say) deliberately create massive unemployment through its fiscal and monetary policies may be given credit for weakening the power of labour and strengthening the power of management. Even then, these policies are held responsible for the low level of investment in British manufacturing industry since the government came into power.

### The Contribution of Macroeconomic Policy

On the surface, a macroeconomic policy which appears to have con-

8  S. Brittan, 'The economy: traumatic rather than radical' in *The Thatcher Years*, a balanced appraisal by the *Financial Times*, 1987.

strained aggregate demand for both goods and labour excessively, which has produced high nominal and real interest rates and an over-valued exchange rate, and which by the abolition of exchange control has diverted British saving and North Sea oil revenue away from investment in the UK to investment overseas, would seem to have been designed to weaken manufacturing industry and the British economy generally rather than strengthen it. This has certainly been the view of the government's critics.

There is no doubt that policy pursued by the Thatcher administration since 1979 has run greatly counter to that advocated by many influential economists (e.g. Lord Kaldor) in the 1960s and 1970s. This held that the way out for the British economy was export-led growth based on an undervalued exchange rate and perhaps subsidized labour costs, emulating, so it was thought, the example of other highly successful countries such as West Germany and Japan. The apparent willingness of the UK authorities to acquiesce in, if not actually contrive, sterling's fall in the 1970s possibly reflected an attempt to implement such a policy; but whether that was so or not, it ended in accelerating inflation and in dismal failure. Of course the parallel drawn with Germany and Japan (by the proponents of export-led growth) was always highly mis-leading: it failed to note that although Germany's and Japan's export success was related to depreciation of their *real* exchange rates, their *nominal* exchange rates remained strong throughout. The bases of success in fact lay in these countries' superior productivity perfor-mance, which enabled competitiveness to be combined with a strong nominal exchange rate, low inflation and rising real wages, rather than the reverse.[9] Advocates of the under valued exchange rate approach often seem to overlook that they are in effect advocating a low real wage strategy that would keep the UK competing in low value-added product areas in which competition from Third World countries is already acute and likely to become more so. In fact, UK export per-formance has been poorest in those high technology and high quality product areas where price competition is less important than non-price competitiveness and where world demand has been increasing fastest.[10] A policy of exchange rate depreciation to maintain price competitive-ness discourages, rather than encourages, British industry from changing its pattern of output in a direction that is necessary if Britain is to join the high productivity, high real wage league.

9 The DM/dollar exchange rate remained stable at roughly DM4 to the dollar until 1968 and then appreciated by about 50% in the following five years. The yen/dollar rate was stable until 1970 and then appreciated by 30%.
10 *Midland Bank Review*, Autumn 1986.

It is in this context, namely, the central role of the exchange rate, that macro-policy under the Thatcher administration must be judged. Admittedly, partly because of the coming on stream of North Sea oil which coincided with a rise in world oil price, and partly because of unintended tightness of monetary policy, the *real* exchange rate initially appreciated too severely. Also, in the early stages of its strategy, the government undoubtedly saw the key role of a strong exchange rate as the major instrument for pulling inflation down rather than as a key element in long term industrial strategy,[11] and it was happy to see the exchange rate fall from the excessively high level of 1979–80. Even so, it rightly stood up to pressure from political opponents, academics and industrialists to embark on a policy of exchange rate depreciation to increase short run competitiveness. By refusing to 'accommodate' rising costs and poor productivity with exchange rate depreciation, macro-policy imposed pressure on industry to raise productivity, lower costs and generally up-market its products. It is significant that many firms whose management were often vociferous in their criticism of government policy with respect to the exchange rate in the early years of the strategy, subsequently achieved productivity improvement and product upgrading to a degree that was almost revolutionary.[12] The example of the car industry in which British Leyland (now Austin Rover) achieved a remarkable turnround, has been cited. The success of Sir John Harvey Jones in raising productivity, lowering costs, raising profits and generally restructuring and repositioning Britain's largest chemical company, as compared with 1979–80, has recently been noted. In the words of *The Times* correspondent, 'He pushed for a high-technology ICI with more activities in newer high-potential businesses.'[13] Perhaps all of this would have been achieved without the spur of an 'overvalued' exchange rate in 1979–80 (of which he appeared to be critical at the time), but it seems unlikely.

The years 1979–81 are generally viewed as a diaster for British manufacturing, but future historians may well judge them less as a period

11 It has been argued that the government should have relied on a more balanced fiscal and monetary approach – tighter fiscal, looser monetary – to pull down inflation since this would put less upward pressure on the exchange rate. Not only does this run counter to criticism affirming that fiscal policy was too tight, it understates the power of a strong exchange rate for pulling down inflation, compared with general demand restriction.

12 *Sunday Times*, 1 Mar. 1987.

13 'Harvey Jones and the rise and rise of ICI', *The Times*, 27 Feb. 1987.

that pulled the Conservative government's record down than as one in which the essential basis for sustained long run improvement in economic performance was laid down. It is hard to overstate the significance of the economic shock of 1979–81, whether one takes the view that in these years UK manufacturing industry was virtually destroyed or, on the contrary, forced to accept changes in its management and work practices which now give it a serious chance to survive. Indeed, although it seems unlikely that the government did in fact favour 'shock' treatment as against 'gradualism' when it first came into office in 1979, it can well be argued that the intractable nature of the UK's problems at the end of the 1970s necessitated shock treatment if the country was to escape from them. Given this view, the government's apparent overdoing of monetary restriction in 1979–81 may have been a blessing in disguise, despite its high cost in terms of unemployment, and the steep fall in UK manufacturing output (16 per cent) which occurred in those years, is, on a long term view, irrelevant. The real test of policy is perhaps still to come, in the performance of British industry as North Sea oil runs out. The evidence of the years since 1981 suggests that UK manufacturing does have a future, and one better than could conceivably have been expected in the traumas of the 1970s.

## The Key Importance of North Sea Oil

It is obvious that a deliberate policy of maintaining a strong 'overvalued' exchange rate in the interest of encouraging a change in industrial structure and a rise in labour and capital productivity, which is necessary if international competitiveness is to be combined with high real wages, would be difficult if not impossible without some short run support to the balance of payments. Fortunately for the Thatcher government and the country, the balance of payments had that support in the shape of North Sea oil revenue.

The government has been variously attacked either for wasting oil revenue in a consumption splurge or for misinvesting it to the disadvantage of the British economy. But as has been made clear in chapter 3 it is evident that oil revenue has not been totally or even largely wasted in a consumption splurge, although no doubt UK real income and consumption have been maintained at a higher level with it than would have been possible without it. By the end of 1986 perhaps half of the rent from the North Sea had been invested in overseas assets, yielding a substantial return in the form of dividends and interest from overseas to the British economy. Naturally, this use of the rent has been attacked on the grounds that it would have been better employed in investment at home rather than overseas, but the issue is very complicated. If, by maintaining and strengthening exchange control or by other means, the investment of oil revenue in overseas assets had been prevented, then either the appreciation of sterling in 1979–80 would have been greater than in fact was the case, with even greater adverse effects on competitiveness and profitability, or domestic spending and imports would have been higher. Presumably the critics of government policy with respect to oil revenue would have preferred the second possibility to the first. Even so, this hasn't prevented some of these same critics from also criticizing the government for the fact that Britain's trade balance in manufacturing went into deficit! It is difficult to see how this could have been avoided if the object of policy had been to prevent net investment overseas, i.e. prevent a surplus appearing in the current account of the balance of payments. In such circumstances, Britain's sudden net surplus on oil account would have had to be offset by a deficit elsewhere – inevitably in manufactures, given their relative importance in the trading account.

As far as domestic investment is concerned, the difficulty lies in identifying precisely where and in which industries investment should be made. If left to the Whitehall bureaucrats, past experience does not suggest that they do this at all well. Indeed, if the object of investing domestically is to ensure that Britain had modern industries capable of stepping into the breach when North Sea oil runs out, some sympathy would be due to those officials and politicians who had to make the choice. It would be asking of them more foresight than they would be likely to possess. Of course, in broad terms, some vital areas for investment can be identified, such as education, research and development, and alternative sources of energy. As will be argued later, the government can be criticized for being slow to act in some of these areas.

In general terms, however, investment should be directed to those areas and industries in which the expected return in highest. Such was the lamentable performance, in terms of rate of return on capital, of large sectors of British industry in the 1970s that investment abroad could seem a preferable alternative, and indeed the return on oil revenue invested abroad has in fact been substantial.

It is sometimes argued that the social return, and not simply the private return, on investment should be taken into account in investment decisions. For example, although the private return on capital invested in British industry might be low, investment would enable otherwise unemployed labour to be brought into employment. Since the social cost of using otherwise unemployed labour is zero or very low, allowance should be made for this when measuring the return on the investment. 'Shadow' pricing labour in this way – i.e. calculating labour costs at opportunity cost to society rather than money costs to the firm – has in fact been employed on a significant scale by British governments since the war: it has provided much of the rationale of regional policy.

However, the policy gives rise to the very real danger that firms and regions become trapped in out-of-date technology, practices and products. The crunch when it comes, as it has to at some point, is then more painful. No doubt an important reason why unemployment rose so much in the 1980s is due to the fact that uneconomic firms and industries were sustained for far too long in the 1960s and 1970s. British industry was suffering less from too little investment than from misdirected investment which yielded low returns. As indicated in chapter 1, the marginal capital-output ratio was higher in the UK than in other industrial countries with superior performance in terms of growth and productivity. At the end of the 1970s, the priority was not to invest more in UK manufacturing but rather to raise the productivity of and return on the existing capital stock. Macroeconomic policy in the 1980s has, consciously or not, been well designed to meet such a priority.

In this connection, the reform of the corporate tax system was most important. The abolition of tax relief on fixed investment – i.e. abolition of a capital subsidy – was a strong incentive to firms to make more efficient use of the existing and future capital stock. It also removed the previous bias towards capital-intensive methods of production and was thus good for employment. At the same time, the cut in the standard rate of corporate tax, from 52 per cent to 35 per cent (although in stages), was a strong incentive for investment. Indeed, once the reforms had fully worked through, the UK looked to be the most attractive country for multinational companies to invest in and pay tax in.

On balance, the contribution of North Sea oil revenue to policy and performance in the 1980s lies less perhaps in the build-up of foreign assets (although these will yield a significant and useful flow of income in foreign exchange that will go a long way to closing the implied gap in the UK's balance of payments as oil runs out) than in the protection it has given to the UK's balance of payments during a period when substantial and needed structural changes in Britain's industry have been taking place. Moreover, although the restructuring of British industry has involved high cost in terms of unemployment, North Sea oil revenue has enabled the country's real income to be maintained at a reasonably high level. As a result, there has possibly been more willingness to accept the necessary structural changes in the economy than would have been the case if less income support had been available.

Summing up at this stage, we can conclude that the stance of macroeconomic policy has been *consistent with* the need to bring about urgently needed changes in the structure and efficiency of British industry. The abandonment of 'demand management' and a determination not to accommodate cost and price raising pressures by excessive monetary expansion and deliberate exchange rate depreciation has undoubtedly improved the supply side performance of the economy. It is difficult to believe that continuation of demand management along the lines of the 1960s and 1970s could have achieved the real productivity improvements witnessed in recent years; indeed, it is by no means certain that demand management could have prevented a substantial rise in unemployment, given the international environment, and it would certainly have been much more inflationary. However, while the government could claim that macro-policy has very broadly provided a *necessary* condition for, at the very least, a start to industrial rejuvenation, it can hardly claim that it has been a sufficient condition; and the government is more vulnerable to an attack for things it didn't do than the things it did do. Hence, in completing our assessment of the government's economic record in its first two terms (1979–87) we refer to four areas where policy has been less than adequate or over delayed.

**Industrial Policy**

In a recent cogently argued book,[14] David Sainsbury and Christopher Smallwood have put a strong case for downplaying conventional macroeconomic policy and for a much more active and positive industrial policy along the lines pursued in other countries, such as Japan, which have been much less enamoured by sophisticated macroeconomic fine tuning. Recognizing that 'industrial policy' has understandably a bad name in the UK – since in the 1960s and 1970s it was associated with maintaining uneconomic firms and industries or involved in the dangerous practice of picking winners – they present a twofold approach: first, a policy for 'making markets work better', and second a set of policies aimed at improving performance at the firm level.

In respect of the first, Sainsbury and Smallwood have in mind a set

14 D. Sainsbury and C. Smallwood, *Wealth Creation – and Jobs* (Public Policy Centre, 1987).

of actions or measures that would increase the competitive pressure on industry to innovate, embrace new technology and keep down costs. These include; first, legislative and other measures that would prevent companies from sharing out markets and customers, from creating monopolies and from adopting predatory pricing policies that eliminate smaller rival companies; second, a public policy that would limit the creation of statutory monopolies and open up existing ones to more competition; and third, an active pursuance of a policy of free trade, thus opening up British industry to foreign competition whilst protecting legitimate British interests abroad.

They rightly point, as has Corelli Barnett in the book referred to earlier, to the fact that British industry became heavily cartelized and protected in the 1930s; and for obvious reasons this was accentuated in the war. Despite a more liberal trading framework established after 1945 and despite the establishment of the Monopolies Commission, the Office of Fair Trading, and the Restrictive Practices Court, the UK is still a long way from having a really competitive environment. The mechanism for promoting more competition, as provided by the three institutions, essentially works in an *ad hoc* case-by-case fashion and has failed to produce a body of case law that can be applied swiftly and generally. Also, in adopting the practice of requiring evidence that the creation of a monopoly or a merger is 'against the public interest' rather than on insisting that evidence should be submitted that the monopoly or merger is 'in the public interest', the mechanism fails to ensure that public as well as private benefits are obtained. Of course, Sainsbury and Smallwood do not want to discourage co-operation in Research and Development, and they admit the case for agreements which permit the orderly running down of excess capacity, although, clearly, these can be taken advantage of by inefficient firms. On the hoary old subject and history of nationalization and denationalization they take the sensible view that competition and liberalization are more important than ownership. Of course the government can claim that it has not been inactive in this area and can claim that its policy of privatization has been a move in the right direction; moreover, it has been giving consideration (the Liesner Committee[15]) to changing the rules and regulations governing mergers and acquisitions. However, a change of ownership *per se* provides no guarantee of more competition: private monopolies are no better than public ones; and it has to be said that government has been kinder to private monopolies and cartels

15 Named after the Deputy Secretary of the Department of Trade and Industry chairing the committee.

than public interest would require. Moreover, where some sort of monopoly position is inevitable, making public sector industry more efficient may be preferable to privatization.

Equally important, and indeed more urgent, are policies to improve performance at the firm or industrial level. Although, as we have seen, there have been significant gains in industrial productivity in recent years, in general British industry still lags behind that in other countries. The reason for the lag lies much more in the poor educational and skill levels of its labour force, in lack of management training, and in the relatively low level of Research and Development and/or its application in large sectors of British industry, than in the conduct of economic policy *per se*.

## Education and Training

In his indictment of Britain's industrial performance Corelli Barnett puts great stress on the failure of the British educational system to produce the skilled labour force that was essential if the country was to remain competitive with other countries.[16] As always, the problem goes back to the Industrial Revolution, when Britain's early industrial superiority was based on a largely uneducated and illiterate labour force. 'Of all the grievous long term handicaps bequeathed to modern Britain by her experience in the first industrial revolution from 1780 to 1850, one of the most pervasive and the most intractable was that of a workforce too largely composed of coolies, with the psychology and primitive culture to be expected of coolies'[17]; and little had changed by the Second World War. The post-war attempt to get to grips with the problem, much lauded at the time – the 1944 Education Act – was a failure. Its overwhelming humanist bias, its emphasis on so-called liberal education and its downplaying of technical education bore no relation to the pressing need to create a skilled industrial workforce. The Act failed to create a nationwide system under a ministry of education which could play a major role in determining curriculum and standards; instead, these important matters were left largely in the hands of local authorities. Not until the mid 1950s was some real attention paid to technical education (the White Paper on Technical Education); and although one or two colleges of advanced technology were established, no real progress was made in injecting appropriate training lower down in the system.

16 Corelli Barnett, *The Audit of War*, ch. 2.
17 Ibid., p. 187.

The failure of the British educational system to produce the right people has of course been documented by a number of important studies. These demonstrate that it is not simply a matter of insufficient technical training: the problems go back into the school system.

In an examination of the question whether important differences exist between the English and the West German schooling system that are likely to bear on productivity differences, Prais and Wagner have no hesitation in concluding that they do: 'the German schooling system provides a broader curriculum, combined with significantly higher levels of mathematical attainment, for a greater proportion of pupils than does the English system: differences are particularly marked at the lower half of the ability range. . . . It is also important that German schools provide more pre-vocational instruction than do English schools, and this has a definite commercial and industrial (not merely "craft") emphasis'.[18] In general there is a stronger link between German schools which helps to co-ordinate the curriculum and to develop teaching material, and there are also stronger links between German schools and vocational education. Detailed examination shows that only 20 per cent of German pupils leave school with no certificate of broad education, and that German pupils are required to reach a reasonable standard in a broad coverage of subjects with stricter requirements for core subjects, including mathematics. Whereas the UK curriculum is heavily weighted to the requirements of university entrance (which is open to relatively few), the German educational system contains a strong intermediate stream with orientation towards scientific, technical and business requirements.

Even where the British system is at its strongest, namely in preparation for university entrance, the curriculum is overspecialized. Whereas British students are required to study three subjects for university entrance, the German system requires five, and even this is less than the seven required in France and the eight to ten in Japan.[19] British children (at least those in England and Wales) are forced to take an early decision about their future education which not only impairs their future career prospects but undoubtedly holds back the supply of engineers, scientists and technologists who not only have the necessary scientific and technical training but are also literate and capable of communicating in foreign languages.

The relative failure of the UK educational system does not stop at the

18 S.J. Prais and K. Wagner, 'Schooling standards in England and Germany: same summary, comparisons bearing on economic performance,' *National Institute Economic Review*, 112 (May 1985), p. 68.

19 Sainsbury and Smallwood, *Wealth Creation – and Jobs*, p. 60.

school level. In another study of training standards in five important occupations, Prais and Wagner demonstrate the inadequacy of the British system of post-school training as compared with that of West Germany. Whilst making all the proper reservations, Prais and Wagner conclude that 'it seems beyond dispute that Germany's successful economy has been well served by its highly developed vocational training system; while Britain's industrial malaise has – at the least – been compounded by inadequate training.'[20] They show that a much larger proportion of the German workforce have attained vocational qualifications at least as high as those obtained by a much smaller proportion of the British workforce. In quantitative terms, the numbers qualifying each year as mechanical fitters, electricians and building craftsmen in Britain are between a half and a third of the corresponding numbers in Germany, as clerical workers (basic correspondence and book-keeping) only about one fifth, and as shopworkers and workers in distributive activities generally, negligible numbers as compared with Germany. Moreover, greater testing of skills under examination conditions – theoretical papers as well as practical tests – is required of the German worker as against the somewhat less demanding monitoring and course assessment applied to the British. In addition, the better preparation at school level in basic arithmetic and mathematics of the German worker is noted.

In general, Germany has a formalized vocational training programme which provides three years of training for all school-leavers for most occupations, closely linked to a system of external examinations. Nothing comparable exists in the UK, although some steps have been taken in recent years (see later). Absence of adequate training cannot be solely laid at the government's door. British industry is also at fault in giving low priority to training, and spending much less on it as a proportion of turnover than do German or Japanese employers.[21]

The results are clear to see. In a study of productivity in 45 matched firms in Britain and West Germany,[22] Daly, Hitchens and Wagner show that labour productivity was on average 63 per cent higher in the German factories as compared with British ones – a conclusion which

20 S.J. Prais and K. Wagner, 'Some practical aspects of human Capital Investment: Training Standards in Five Occupations in Britain and Germany' *National Institute Economic Review*, 105 (Aug. 1983), p. 63.

21 Sainsbury and Smallwood, *Wealth Creation – and Jobs*, p. 6.

22 A. Daly, D. Hitchens and K. Wagner, 'Productivity, machinery and skills in a sample of British and German manufacturing plants: results of pilot enquiry', *National Institute Economic Review*, 111 (Feb. 1985).

is supported by more widely based figures derived from consenses of production which show that German output per employee in manufacturing as a whole is about 50 per cent higher than in Britain. While this differential has probably been narrowed in recent years by developments referred to earlier, nonetheless the facts do suggest that the UK's post-war preoccupation with maintaining full employment at almost any level of productivity was allocated an excessive priority.

Despite the glaring deficiencies of Britain's educational and training system, which underlies Britain's inferior economic performance, the Thatcher government was slow to act. Not until 1986 were decisive measures taken to improve the system. Admittedly some preliminary steps were taken earlier. Sir Keith Joseph (Minister of Education in the first Thatcher administration) can be congratulated for drawing the attention of the British people to differences between British and European schooling that could account for differences in economic performance. For example, the Centre for Policy Studies published *Lessons from Europe*, a comparison of British and West European schooling. Later, in November 1985, the Department of Education and Science published '*Selected National Eduational Systems*' which provided potted descriptions of education in France, Italy, Japan, West Germany, the Netherlands and the US. This publicity initiative followed the failure of earlier proposals put forward by Mark Carlisle, predecessor of Sir Keith Joseph, to introduce limited changes in the school curriculum. These proposed that 10 per cent of school time be allocated to mathematics, 10 per cent to English, 10–20 per cent to science subjects, and 10 per cent to a foreign language. Despite the limited nature of the proposal, it foundered on the opposition of local authority autonomy and teacher antagonism. 'All that remained were some "enigmatic" generalities about the need for balance and breadth in the curriculum, high standards, equal opportunities and the like.'[23] Thus, in its first term of office (1979–83) the government showed little or no determination to force educational reform through.

In its second term of office, further official documents appeared, culminating in the White Paper on Better Schools (Cmnd. 9469, March 1985) which proposed changes in public examinations in respect of coverage and national criteria for main subjects. But a real attempt to introduce a national curriculum containing a set number of hours for the core subjects – English, mathematics, science, etc. – for all children up to the age of 16, complemented by staged testing to ensure

23 Prais and Wagner, 'Schooling standards in England and Germany', p. 70.

motivation and performance, had to wait the arrival of Kenneth Baker and the Education Act of 1986 – that is, after the government had been in power for seven years. Thus, while at the time of writing there are intentions for the future (and the government's re-election will put those intentions to the test), little or no improvement to Britain's school system was made in the government's first two terms of office.

Turning now to technical and vocational training, the government can claim to have introduced or expanded a large number of programmes, particularly since April 1983. These include the Youth Training Scheme and the Technical and Vocational Education Initiative aimed at school-leavers; and, under the heading of Adult Training, various programmes to meet national and local needs and to help the employed, unemployed, and self-employed, as well as employers, to enhance skills. (Table 6.9 lists the schemes with their objectives and conditions, and table 6.10 records the numbers covered by them.) Of course, there can be little doubt that the introduction of these schemes has been at least partly motivated by the need to absorb at least temporarily the growing numbers of unemployed. Moreover, owing to a deficiency of information on the national demand for and supply of particular skills, there is some doubt as to whether training is not simply being provided in skills already in good supply.[24] A delay in introducing a national system of training standards is also a serious impediment to matching supply and demand for skills effectively. Undoubtedly the whole programme suffers from the haste with which it has been introduced. Nonetheless, the government can rightly claim credit for a significant if belated initiative.

A further necessary step was taken in the 1987 budget, in providing tax relief on expenditure by firms on training, although it does not go far enough. Sainsbury and Smallwood have suggested a remissible tax approach by which firms spending more on training than a pre-assessed amount would receive 100 per cent tax relief on the excess, while those spending less would have to pay a 100 per cent tax on the deficiency. However, the 'free rider' problem remains, namely, that firms not spending on training can still derive benefit from the spending of firms which do; and there could be advantage in making a levy on all firms to finance industrial training programmes.

Of course it is not only workers who require training: a glaring deficiency in British industrial life is training for management. Only a small proportion (30 per cent) of British managers receive training

24 Department of Employment and Manpower Services Commission: Adult Training Strategy. Report by the Comptroller and Auditor General.

initially or on an ongoing basis during their working lives, and only a minute proportion have a business degree or management qualification. A study of management education in five countries by Kempner indicates that Britain's major competitors spend more on management education than does Britain, although not necessarily in the same manner.[25] In the US the typical channel is through study for an MBA (Master of Business Administration) at major universities, in Japan company-based education schemes are the principal means, and in France the *grand écoles* play an important role. Although West Germany does not have business schools of the American kind, a large number of its engineers and technologists receive managerial education as part of their first degrees. It is true that three major business schools were created in Britain during the 1960s and that encouragement was given to the establishment of postgraduate courses in business and management, but it is evident that governments in Britain, including the Thatcher one, have not tackled the problem with the urgency required.

### Research and Development

To Britain's failure to educate and train its management and workforce must be added its failure to devote sufficient resources to research and development, particularly in the non-defence sectors of the economy. The proportion of GDP spent on Research and Development in the UK is not significantly different from that spent in other major industrial countries, but a higher proportion is allocated to defence (nearly 50 per cent) than in other countries. As a result, non-defence R. & D. as a proportion of GDP is lower than in those countries.[26] Moreover, owing to a bias in favour of the glamorous 'big science' projects such as nuclear energy and aerospace, the pay-off in terms of industrial performance and competitiveness has been poor.

Of course, if the government feels it necessary to devote a substantial part of the UK's output to defence – as have all previous post-war governments – then the policy has to be supported by appropriate defence research, but the implications for the drain on scientists and skilled manpower should be recognized and appropriate measures

25 T. Kempner 'Education for management in five countries: myth and reality', *Journal of General Management*, 9/2 (Winter 1983–4).
26 1.6% compared with the US 1.9%, France 1.8%, West Germany 2.6%, Japan 2.5% – *National Science Foundation*.

taken in the field of education and training and in non-defence R. & D. expenditure so that the UK's non-defence industrial performance is not adversely affected. Also, it has for long been appreciated that Britain's scientists contribute more to basic research than to the transfer and diffusion of new technology. The result is that in practice other countries benefit more from British research than Britain does itself.

Sainsbury and Smallwood suggest three courses of action: first, a conscious and deliberate attempt to align more closely the country's research effort with industrial objectives; second, the allocation of more resources into the diffusion of already known technology; and third, an active campaign to import foreign technology. Of course, although the onus is on the government to promote initiatives of this and other kinds, in the last resort – as with training – responsibility lies with industry itself: only industry can take effective action to promote and pay for the research and technology necessary for it to compete abroad. But government can provide financial encouragement, both to the providers and to the users of research. For example, British universities, which have been financially squeezed in recent years and are now more ready to direct their research efforts to the needs of industry than was the case in their 'ivory tower' years, should now be given less stick and more carrot, in the form of government matching of funds received from industry for research work. Also, although the government's decision in 1984 to abolish tax allowances on capital expenditure (in exchange for a substantial cut in basic corporate tax) was certainly correct and has been justified by recent developments, an exception could well be made for R. & D. expenditure. Industry-funded research at universities could be made deductible for corporation tax, as could in-house expenditure, subject to vertification. Whichever way it is done, the need for action with respect to R. & D. is urgent, and the government can be rightly blamed for giving it insufficient priority.

## Unemployment

The lack of education and vocation training of Britain's labour force has undoubtedly contributed to the country's serious unemployment problem. The long term unemployed have lacked the skills that would have enabled them to secure new jobs in place of those lost. Moreover, lack of occupational mobility has in many cases been compounded by geographical immobility. While sociological factors have been important, a root cause lies in decades of rent control, which has virtually eliminated the supply of private rented accommodation. Planning restrictions on the use of land, particularly in the prosperous south, have constrained public and private house-building, thereby maintaining house prices in areas where jobs have been available above the level affordable by those willing to seek jobs away from the depressed areas.

Of course, the Thatcher government is not responsible for the deplorable state of Britain's educational system and housing market which is the product of years of neglect and bad policy pursued by earlier governments, but the state of those markets made a mockery of the government's initial reliance on the workings of the labour market to deal with unemployment. As noted in chapter 6, the government has been gradually forced into taking special measures to deal with the unemployment problem, and further such measures are likely to be required in its third term of office. Although a major initiative on education and training appears to be in the offing,[27] there seems to be a considerable reluctance to get to grips with the housing market, without which unemployment is likely to remain an acute regional problem.

## Final Assessment

What then should be the final assessment of the first two terms of Mrs Thatcher's handling of the economy? And in the light of the results, what is the outlook for the future?

In the light of the massive problems facing the UK economy at the end of the 1970s, the government was right to abandon short run demand management and to concentrate on improving the supply side performance of the economy. Although fiscal and particularly monetary policy was possibly too tight – probably unintentionally so – in the first eighteen months of the administration, resulting in an appreciation of the real exchange rate by more than could be expected from the benefit of North Sea oil alone, the impact on the economy was not all adverse: in the long run, it may well have been beneficial. The pressure on industry to raise efficiency and control costs – resulting in a huge shake-out of labour – undoubtedly set the scene for a massive improvement in performance which would not have been obtained with a more gradualist approach. This is not meant to deny the serious social costs in terms of massive unemployment, but given the parlous state of much of British industry in the 1970s it is doubtful whether large social

27 The post-election Conservative party conference affirmed educational reform as the government's most important objective in its third term.

costs could have been avoided if improvement was to be made. North Sea oil was a tremendous assistance since it substantially protected real incomes in the country in the face of needed structural change. However, while initial tax changes – such as the immediate lowering of the highest marginal rates of taxes from 83 per cent to 60 per cent – were in the right direction, equity and efficiency grounds required that 'perks' and other personal tax allowances be reduced at the same time. While there was a strong case for reducing marginal tax rates, the case for reducing average tax rates was a good deal less pressing.

Since 1981, macro-policy has been sensible and well balanced. The government was right to maintain the fiscal side of the MTFS, but right also to abandon wider money supply targets when it was evident that institutional and other factors were complicating their interpretation and when other evidence was suggesting that monetary policy was too tight. The government was right to accept a fall in the exchange rate from the impossibly high level of 1980, and right also to allow a further fall in the rate following the fall in the price of oil in 1985. But it was also right not to give into pressures for a policy of exchange rate depreciation and undervaluation to promote export-led growth. Although under pressure to join the European Monetary System (EMS), the government's caution on this issue was understandable, at least until oil price fell to a more sustainable level. Since mid 1986, sterling seems to have been made an informal member of the system, a policy seemingly directed at keeping a close link with the Deutschmark.[28] Although it is possible that a formal link would have permitted a lower level of interest rates *on average* in the UK, it cannot be said that non-membership has as yet been a major disadvantage to the UK. The chancellor's drive to achieve a more stable exchange rate system internationally[29] is, however, undoubtedly welcome.

The appropriateness of macro-policy after 1981 is demonstrated by the good performance of the economy since then. GDP growth has averaged about 3 per cent per annum (the longest period of sustained growth since the 1960s) and manufacturing growth not much less;[30] labour productivity growth in manufacturing industry has averaged nearly 6 per cent per annum (after allowing for cyclical upturn – 4.8 per cent); inflation has fallen to around 4 per cent, and since 1985 has

28  Since mid 1986, the DM/sterling exchange rate has remained within the band 2.8–3.0, being closer to 3.0 for most of 1987.

29  In his address at the annual meeting of the IMF in 1987.

30  GDP increased by over 4% in 1987, and manufacturing production by over 5%.

been largely productivity driven (see p. 124), and, since reaching a peak in October 1986, unemployment has fallen by over 400,000.[31] The balance of payments has been in surplus through most of the period and substantial overseas assets have been built up.

The counter-arguments emphasizing the failure of manufacturing output to grow since 1979, the fact that the UK now has a trade deficit in manufactures for the first time in its history, and the massive rise in unemployment, are all superficially understandable. But the first of these counter-arguments puts too much weight on the first two years of the government's strategy and too little on the sustained performance since 1981. The second seems to overlook totally the fact that also for the first time in its history the UK became a substantial net exporter of energy, at a time when the real price of it increased massively (it could also be noted that the UK moved from importing over 50 per cent of its food to barely 30 per cent), so that it was unlikely to be able to maintain the same trade position in manufactures. While the third counter-argument has to be taken very seriously indeed, since unemployment on the present scale is certainly unacceptable, it also has to be noted that unemployment has risen massively in most industrial countries; in some of them, not significantly less than in the UK. This suggests that domestic policy in the UK was by no means the only factor. Factors that also have to be taken into account are the impact of the oil price rise on the full employment real wage and the subsequent displacement of labour by capital; a technological revolution which is clearly displacing labour (and capital) in many industries worldwide; and growing competition from newly industrializing countries, particularly in industrial sectors that have played a major role in the older countries' post-war development.

However, the question remains whether the improvement in British productivity and industrial performance generally, and the fall in inflation, could not have been obtained with less social cost in terms of unemployment; and incomes policies have been favoured by some opponents of policy. But even if it had wished to – which it clearly did not – the government could not have introduced incomes policies of the old kind in 1979–80 since the trade union movement had made clear its opposition to them; and that opposition appears to remain today. Tax-based policies may be the solution, as suggested by some economists, but there are considerably doubts about their workability, particularly with respect to the public sector industries and services which have often been at the heart of the UK's labour problems.

31 Unemployment fell by another 500,000 through 1988.

Nonetheless, the problem of the long term unemployment is becoming an increasingly urgent one, particularly as we should not expect manufacturing industry, no matter how well it does in the future, to make much contribution, if any, to the future growth of employment; and the government can well be criticzed for delay in targeting special measures to deal with it.

Linked with the problem of unemployment are the inadequate skills and training levels of much of Britain's industrial labour force; and as has been made clear earlier in this chapter, the government can be legitimately criticized for lack of urgency in dealing with this aspect, as well as the Research and Development aspect, of Britain's long term industrial problems. Industrial strategy has had a bad name in the past, but the greatly improved macroeconomic position of the British economy does provide a better base for well-directed industrial policies in future. Having stopped the rot, the government is now in a much better position to take more positive steps of a micro nature to promote growth.

What then is the outlook for the British economy?

Although deep and fundamental problems remain, the government can rightly claim that the economy is now better positioned for sustained growth than has been the case for many years. A further few years of 2.5–3 per cent growth seem assured.[31] If achieved, disparaging reference to the years of 1979–81 will become less and less relevant. Critics will have to concentrate on the decade of the 1980s as a whole. There are fears constantly stressed by the opponents of present policy that Britain faces a balance of payments crisis now that oil price has fallen and oil output has peaked out. In fact, the balance of payments is not an immediate problem, even though with a much lower oil price the current account is likely to move into and remain in moderate deficit for the next few years; but this will create no problem, given the UK's large stock of overseas assets (amounting to £115 billion (net) at the end of 1986), not to mention the UK's growing attractiveness to foreign investment.[32] Moreover it can reasonably be expected that, years of 2.5–3 per cent growth seem assured.[32] If achieved, disparaging foreign investment.[33] Moreover it can reasonably be expected that, will be stimulated.[34] Manufacturing, slimmed down but greatly more

32 London Business School economic forecast.

33 In the first six months of 1987, Japanese investment in UK securities was running at an annualized rate of over $5 billion – *Shearson Lehman Securities, UK Economic Research Studies*, 4 Sept. 1987.

34 See Geoffrey Maynard, 'The UK's manufacturing deficit doesn't matter', *Financial Times*, 29 Jan. 1986.

efficient than it was in 1979, is now in a better position to take oil's place. Inflation is not yet fully defeated, however, and may never be by West Germany's standards; but with continuation of cautious fiscal and monetary policies, as established in the MTFS and implemented yet again in the 1987 budget, it should not present the problems it did in the 1970s. [35]. Unemployment remains the most urgent short term problem and will require specific treatment by government. Given that, there seems need for continuation of policies aimed at improving the supply side performance of the economy, the most urgent of which seems to be reform of the educational system and of the structure of personal taxation. While some short run and limited demand management can hardly be avoided, a return to the exaggerated policies of the 1960s and 1970s would seem both unnecessary and unwelcome. Fortunately, the British people seem to have taken this view in the election of June 1987.

35 Unfortunately, the government abandoned its cautious monetary and fiscal policy in 1987–8, leading to a sharp rise in inflation and putting at risk the undoubted gains of its medium term strategy.

# Index

fiscal policy
  expansionist 29, 36–9, 74, 83, 105–6, 112
  Keynesian 2, 8–11, 35–8
  restrictive 97–8, 104, 106
  Thatcherism 30–1, 35–40, 63–9, 72–4, 79, 96n., 103–12, 156; critique of 98, 104–12, 158n., 171
France
  economic performance 27, 94–5, 152
  management training 169
Free Forward Fares Scheme 139, 144
Friedman, Milton 11, 32

GDP 23, 27, 39
  money 32–5, 36–7, 63, 73, 79–80, 83, 101–2, 131
  rise in 47, 63, 69, 72–3, 76, 89, 94, 146n., 172
Gansden, R. 120n.
Germany
  economic performance 94–5, 152–3, 157, 175
  education system 165–7
  management training 169
  post-war reconstruction 26–7
  trade union membership 136
gradualism, rejection of 98, 159, 171
growth
  export-led 21, 97, 157, 172
  rate of, and Keynesian policies 7, 12–13, 18, 26–8, 172
growth rate, capacity output 105

Hall, S.G. and Henry, S.G.B. 123
Harvey Jones, John 158
Heath, Edward, macroeconomic policy 2n., 11–12, 30n.
Henry, S.G. 5n.
Hicks, J. R. 6
hire purchase control 2n., 31
housing
  costs 130, 137, 146, 171
  post-war 26

IBELs, *see* liabilities, interest-bearing eligible
imports
  controls on 30
  food 96n.
  and North Sea oil revenues 54, 56, 93
*In Place of Strife* 86
income, distribution 59
incomes policy
  abandonment of vii, 30, 43, 103, 173
  demand for 132–5
  Keynesian 3–5, 22–3, 24, 29–30
Industrial Relations Act 1971 86–7
industry
  performance 128–9, 164, 171, 173
  restructuring 161–2
inflation
  adjustment for 105–10
  control of: Keynesian policies 3–5, 7, 8, 24, 27, 29; Thatcherism vii, 30, 32, 40–2, 59, 65, 68–70, 73, 76, 83, 90–2, 93, 100–4, 124, 172–3, 175
  cost push 3
  growth in 9–13, 20, 22–3, 29, 39, 59, 97, 111, 118–19, 122, 131, 146–7, 157
  productivity-gap 124
  world rate 8–9
  *see also* unemployment
insiders/outsiders 126–7, 130, 135
interest rates
  Keynesian policy 2, 6, 9–11, 18, 22
  and money supply 33–7, 40, 60, 63, 66, 68, 74, 76, 79–83, 98–104, 172
  and Thatcherist policies 106–12, 115, 128, 157
  under Heath 13
International Aeradio, privatization of 85
International Monetary Fund, Britain's debt to 21, 23, 29

*Index by Meg Davies*